# Unlearning discrimination in the early years

# Unlearning discrimination in the early years

Babette Brown

**Trentham Books**

## Dedication

**To my very special grandchildren: Holly, Daniel, Philani, Emma, Sam, Natasha and Katle**

## Acknowledgements

I would like to thank Sue Adler, Molly Arenstein, Cathy, David, Fiona, Jenny, Mannie and Peter Brown, Louise Derman-Sparks, Brendah Gaine, Gillian Klein, Jane Lane, Liz Lawrence, Lorna MacNab and Greta Sandler for the books, ideas and emotional support they generously offered and for willingly and critically reading the manuscript.

Thank you also to NES Arnold and the Equality Learning Centre for loaning the dolls that appear on the cover, the Spinal Injuries Association for permission to use the poem, 'Tomorrow I Am Going To Rewrite the English Language' by Lois Keith and to Learning Development Aids for permission to use the extract from *Turn Your School Around* by Jenny Mosley.

First published in 1998 by Trentham Books Limited

Reprinted 1999

Trentham Books Limited
Westview House
734 London Road
Oakhill
Stoke on Trent
Staffordshire
England ST4 5NP

**British Cataloguing in Publication Data**
A catalogue record for this book is available from the British Library
ISBN 1 85856 122 1
(hb ISBN 1 85856 121 3)

Designed and typeset by Trentham Print Design Ltd., Chester and printed in Great Britain by The Cromwell Press Ltd., Wiltshire

# Contents

## GAUTENG PROVINCIAL GOVERNMENT
MEC FOR EDUCATION

3rd February 1998

Dear Babette,

I was delighted to learn that you are the 1997 winner of The Guardian Jerwood Award and I may say that no person is more deserving of this honour.

Congratulations, and you must be thrilled that all your years of hard work and perservance, often in the face of tough opposition and criticism, have at last been recognised so publicly. I wish you continued, and increasing, success with your Network, and hope that your campaign to influence Government policy on equality issues bears fruit. You have achieved so much, and we in South Africa are tremendously proud of your success.

Best wishes

**MARY METCLAFFE**
**MEC FOR EDUCATION**
**GAUTENG**

# Foreword

If you choose the path of undoing discrimination in early years care and education, then this book is for you. Its wise, informative discussion is exceptionally clear and easy to read. Ideas are presented with a simplicity that makes even the most complex concepts accessible. If you are reading for the first time about the impact of prejudice and discrimination on early years care and education programs – and what you can do about it – you will discover a wealth of information and insight. If you are already a worker in the field of equity education, the discussion of the range of dynamics of the various forms of discrimination will deepen your understanding of the tasks integral to implementing life-enhancing early years programs for all.

Alice Walker, a favourite author of mine, once wrote: 'Keep in mind always the present you are constructing. It should be the future you want'.[1] I know of no person whose life better exemplifies that call than Babette Brown, the author of this book. In her professional, personal and community life, Babette has devoted her many gifts to the awesome tasks of eradicating the societal and individual barriers that prevent too many young children from experiencing nurturing, quality care and education programs. She is a role model and inspiration to many, including me.

I first became acquainted with Babette when she invited me to speak at a conference sponsored by EYTARN (Early Years Anti Racist Network) – an organisation she founded and led for many years. Since then we have come together on many occasions – in the United Kingdom, in the Netherlands and Belgium, and in South Africa. These treasured times taught me how important international relationships are to the work of eliminating prejudice and discrimination. Each country has its own unique history, conditions, cultures that shape early years work in general, and anti-discrimination work in particular. At the same time, certain dynamics seem to cut across national boundaries. In learning from each other we gain increased clarity about the dynamics of our specific work and greater understanding of shared issues and challenges. Reading *Unlearning Discrimination in the Early Years* was just that kind of experience for me.

The United States of America pledge of allegiance includes the phrase 'liberty and justice for all', yet our society is very far from putting this fundamental principle into daily practice. Our children daily face profound double messages about diversity and justice – in their homes, in their child care centres and preschools, in their communities, in the media. As I wrote in the Introduction of my book *Anti-Bias Curriculum: Tools For Empowering Young Children*[2]:

> Children are aware very young that colour, language, gender and physical ability are connected with power and privilege. Racism, sexism, and other forms of systemic discrimination have a profound influence on their developing sense of self and others... All children are harmed. On the one hand, struggling against bias that declares a person inferior because of gender, race, ethnicity, disability, or class sucks energy from and undercuts a child's full development.
>
> On the other hand, learning to believe they are superior because they are white, or male, or able-bodied, or rich, de-humanises and distorts reality for growing children, even while they may be receiving the benefits of institutional privilege.

As the 21st century fast approaches, the challenge of ending discrimination of all kinds remains crucial to our world's healthy survival. As early years practitioners we have a particular responsibility in this critical work because children come to us at the very beginning of their development of attitudes about themselves and others. We have pressing choices to make. We can guide young children's construction of a strong identity and teach them to value all the varied ways people are and live; or we can allow them to build an unstable self-identity based on ignorance and fear of people different from themselves. We can create early years programs that genuinely practice the basic ethic of our profession – to nurture the fullest development of all children; or we can continue to disempower some groups of children while teaching other groups to maintain privilege for themselves.

Like children, adults learn new ideas and behaviours by making mistakes, getting help from others, thinking about what they did, and trying again. Moreover, because learning discrimination in early years care and education is at heart about social change, it will not be easy. Our work 'may meet with resistance – from other teachers, from parents, from administrators – and from one's own ambivalence and discomforts'.[3] All social change takes commitment, persistence, courage and a vision of the future we want. I cannot imagine a more exciting and satisfying way of being an early years educator than joining in the work of creating a more caring and just world for all children.

Louise Derman-Sparks
*Pacific Oaks College, Pasadena, CA, UDA*
*February 1998*

## References

1.   Walker, A. (1969) *Temple of my familiar.* NY: Harcourt Brace Jovanovich. p.236
2.   Derman-Sparks, L. & the ABC Task Force. (1989) Washington, DC: NAEYC ix
3.   op.cit. x

# Introduction

This book draws on my experiences as a nursery school teacher, a tutor on an NNEB course and as a mother and grandmother, to contribute to policy and practice that values young children and treats them all with equal concern and respect. I hope that readers will be motivated to reflect, adapt and constantly monitor existing good practice, challenge discriminatory attitudes and behaviour and actively contribute to the difficult but exciting process of challenging racism and other forms of discrimination.

As educators we know that young children are profoundly influenced by their families and by the communities in which they live but we may be less aware of the part that social factors like racism, sexism, class, homophobia and ablism play in their lives. These social inequalities are all intricately linked together, influencing one another and interweaving to form a web. Although this inter-connection is highlighted throughout the book, the main focus is on challenging racism. The reason is personal – I was for eleven and a half years the Co-ordinator of the Early Years Trainers Anti-Racist Network, EYTARN, which runs inservice anti-racist training days for childminders and early years staff, organises annual conferences and produces training publications on a range of equality issues.

The anti-discriminatory principles underpinning the book include:

- Educational practice based on equality and justice is good educational practice and involves developing empowering relationships built on trust, respect and an appreciation of diversity.

1

- Racism and other social inequalities are deeply rooted in British history and still profoundly affect the lives of children and their families. These inequalities were created by and are being perpetuated by people so they can be changed by people.

- All children are entitled to equality of access and treatment and to opportunities to learn from a stimulating and culturally appropriate curriculum.

- We have a responsibility to support children's early learning and to help them unlearn the prejudices and discriminatory attitudes they absorb from the world around them.

The way we interact with children is at the heart of good educational practice. Carefully observing them is an important part of this process, as Mary Jane Drummond (1995:92) explains:

> First and foremost when we watch young children, we can see them learning. And young children's learning is so rich, fascinating, varied, surprising, enthusiastic and energetic, that to see it taking place before one's very eyes, every day of the week, is one of the great rewards of being with young children, as educator, carer or parent. .... It opens our eyes to the astonishing capacity of young children to learn and to the crucial importance of these first few years of our children's lives. But when we watch children we do more than simply marvel at their intellectual and emotional energy; we can also learn, by watching carefully and thinking things over, to understand what we see. .... Everything we know about children's learning imposes on us an obligation to do whatever we can to foster and develop it.

We are under pressure to provide a more 'academic' environment for young children but the focus on subject divisions, formal learning and desirable outcomes interfers with and runs counter to the holistic and experiential way in which they learn. Rumbold (1990:9) pointed out that:

> For the early years educator, therefore, the process of education – how children learn – how children are encouraged to learn – is as important as, and inseparable from, the content – what they learn.

We believe that this principle must underlie all curricula for the under fives. ... We believe that the aims of the curriculum will most readily be achieved where skilled and knowledgable staff:

a. hold high expectations of all children, not limited by stereotyped views about class, cultural background, sex or special educational needs;

b. value parents as their children's first educators and as active partners in the continuing process of education.

Children can become active, enthusiastic and independent learners if, as their educators, we value their cultures and communities, and understand how racism and other social inequalities influence their lives. With our guidance and support children can, as this example illustrates, actively challenge unfairness.

A group of 6 year old children were looking through a toy catalogue. They told their teacher that they thought that it wasn't fair because there were no pictures of Black children or any showing girls building or climbing. It was agreed that they should write a letter to the manufacturer. They got no reply so they wrote again. This letter was also unacknowledged. The disappointed children enthusiastically agreed with a parent who suggested that they should draw up a petition. Children, staff and parents signed and it was sent off. To the children's delight the company replied that in future pictures in the catalogue would be more carefully chosen.

Experiences like these help children to stand up for what they think is right and to realise how difficult and how satisfying changing something can be.

## A way forward

The pressure under which we work can leave us feeling that we have neither the time nor the energy to confront social inequalities like racism, sexism and class discrimination. However, if anti-discriminatory practice *is* good practice do we in fact have a choice? Can we treat each child with equal concern if we don't appreciate the powerful effect of stereotypical thinking and behaviour on policy and practice? Can our curriculum meet the needs of each child if it is culturally inappropriate and based on discriminatory principles? Can we have discussions around racist, sexist, class or homophobic issues that arouse passionate feelings if we don't trust, respect and listen to one another?

The first step might be to take a long hard look to see whether our inter-actions with children and parents are unconsciously influenced by stereotypical thinking. Do we tend to expect Asian girls to be quiet and submissive, for instance? The next step is to observe children carefully. Do we know whether the children who are perceived as being different are enduring name-calling or physical abuse? Do we actively intervene by comforting and supporting them? Do we help the perpetrators to appreciate the consequences of their words and/or actions by taking a firm, supportive approach? The third step involves examining the definition and content of the curriculum and how it is presented to the children. Are we motivating them by building on the knowledge and experiences they bring from home and encouraging them to work and play collaboratively?

Looking at our own attitudes and practice in this way is essential. But it is not enough. We also need continually to review and, where neces-sary, change institutional policies and practices to ensure that everyone is receiving equal treatment. The Swann Report (1985:29) emphasised the importance of confronting institutional racism:

> We believe that institutional racism is just as much a cause for concern as the prejudiced attitudes which some individuals may hold since the establishment, in this way, of racism within the 'system' itself can serve to reinforce, to magnify and to perpetuate such attitudes even where individual attitudes may be open to change ... We believe that institutional change and changing indivi-dual attitudes are of equal importance and have complementary roles to play in achieving the overall shift in emphasis and outlook which we believe to be essential in relation to today's multi-racial society.

Practical ways in which we can counter institutional practices and policies that are discriminatory include:

• evaluating and regularly monitoring each stage of the process by which students and staff are recruited and selected

• ensuring that once staff are appointed they all have equal promotion opportunities

• checking the procedures by which children are admitted into playgroups, nurseries and schools.

## Terms matter: Black people and White people

There is some controversy about whom the term Black includes. I am using it in its political sense to refer to people of African, Caribbean or Asian origins who experience racism and to those of Arab, Cypriot, or Latin American backgrounds who also experience prejudice and differential treatment because of their ethnicity. This political definition of Black was formulated to unite people of diverse origins and cultures in the fight against racism and at the same time to reflect the reality that various ethnic groups are affected even though they are not equally targeted. Acknowledging that all these groups experience racism entails recognising the vast differences in their cultural patterns and life-styles. However, this usage is not acceptable to all those concerned. Some do not see themselves as allies in a struggle against racism, possibly because of their own racism. The term White is used here also in its political sense, to refer to people in Britain whose skin colour indicates a European ancestry. Although they do not experience racism because of their skin colour some people of, for example, Irish and Jewish backgrounds do experience prejudice and discrimination.

## Terms matter: racism

There is no question that racism exists but that there are distinct races of people is biologically invalid. 'Scientific' theories which classified people according to their 'race' were repudiated more than 40 years ago and few scientists today accept that there are biological grounds for distinguishing one group of people from another. They argue (e.g. Rose, 1985) that differences between people within a particular 'race' are greater than those between people of different 'races'. And yet, although the notion of biologically separate races has no scientific foundation, the concept of race continues to be widely used to justify racism. In Britain it is based on the belief that the intellect, cultures, religions and life-styles of Black people are inferior to those of White people. Racism is expressed through individual attitudes and practices as well as through institutional policies and procedures, even when operated by fair-minded individuals. The perceived 'inferiority' of Black people – not the unequal distribution of wealth, power and privilege – is seen to account for their inability to take advantage of the opportunities that a democratic society offers them. The term racism is used in this book to refer to the deeply rooted, but groundless, belief that certain groups are biologically inferior to others and as a consequence have poorer job opportunities, health, housing and education. Physical and cultural differences between people do not cause racism any more than the anatomical differences between men and women are the cause of sexism.

## Terms matter: culture

The concept of culture is closely related to but separate from that of race. It includes everything that contributes to the life of a group of people, from the objects in their daily experiences to their customs and beliefs, but the way in which each family practices their culture varies. Cultures change and continually influence each other. In fact, because culture is closely related to class, many aspects of British middle class culture are common to both White and Black middle class groups and there are likewise similarities among Black and White working class families.

## Terms matter: sexism

Sexism stems from attitudes and practices based on the belief that a person's gender automatically limits and defines her/his abilities and activities, determines her/his capabilities and behaviour and how she/he should be valued. This way of thinking is likely to be re-enforced if women's achievements in, for example, history, science and literature are ignored, if the male pronoun 'he' is the only one used, if sexist language is accepted and if boys are regarded as active leaders and girls as passive followers. Sexism dehumanises men and boys as well as women and girls. But although it impoverishes both sexes by limiting horizons and restricting choices, girls and women suffer most from the notion of male superiority. Men generally have more power than women, frequently justified in terms of women's alleged 'inferiority' and their accomplishments are often expressed in patronising tones. The upheaval of the two world wars provided opportunities for women to reveal their abilities in jobs they had previously not been allowed to undertake. Attitudes about what is considered appropriate for women to do have changed dramatically. Do you know that before the First World War secretaries were all men because it was believed that typewriters would somehow take away women's femininity? It is true that there is a greater awareness of women's rights today but sexism continues to influence the quality of women's and girls' lives and their life chances.

## Terms matter: homophobia

Homophobia rests on the assumption that heterosexuality, i.e. the emotional and sexual relationship between men and women, is 'normal' and 'natural' and that homosexuality, i.e. the emotional and sexual relationships between people of the same sex, is 'abnormal' and 'unnatural'. The term lesbian refers to relationships between women and gay to those between men. People may be heterosexual and lesbian/gay at different times in their lives. Lesbians and gay men face harassment and abuse. They may be discriminated against when, for example, they seek council housing and they may be prevented from working with children.

## Terms matter: ablism

Ablism is based on the concept of what is considered 'normal' by people who are 'able bodied'. It is not their impairment which prevents disabled people from achieving a reasonable standard of living but attitudes and policies which deny them equal rights and opportunities. For example, not being able to walk is an impairment, but lack of mobility is a disability which could be corrected by providing many more lifts and ramps. Rieser (1992:331) suggests that the reason why discrimination and prejudice directed at people with disabilities have not been generally challenged is because negative attitudes and fear are so deeply rooted that most people are not even aware that they hold such views. He describes his own painful experiences as a child and teenager:

> It was the indirect avoidance of me, the whispering, the staring looks that I couldn't hit out at, that were far more damaging. I was not often allowed to forget my body, being the butt of jokes and jostled and pushed in corridors or on the stairs.

## Terms matter: Travellers

Most Travellers, (this term is preferred to Gypsies) in Britain are either Romany or Celtic. Increased urbanisation and land development have drastically restricted stopping places and they are constantly evicted by Councils and private landowners. Although large numbers live in houses they retain their traditional cultural practices. According to Brian Foster (1993) these include maintaining extended family networks and community contacts, a positive attitude to mobility and a tradition of self-education. For centuries they have been discriminated against and they continue to face prejudice and harassment even though they are covered by the incitement to racial hatred provisions of the Public Order Act, and 'Gypsies' are a distinct racial group within the meaning of the 1976 Race Relations Act.

## The road ahead

Most of us who are working with students or with young children and their parents find the task fulfilling, enjoyable, stressful and exhausting. Although the job we are doing is of such great importance and has such far-reaching consequences, it does not receive the acknowledgment and appreciation it deserves. When implementing anti-discriminatory practice we may meet hostility from people who don't want change or those who are frustrated at the slow pace of change. Experiencing the liberating and empowering process of personal change is energising but it is also demanding and difficult. We struggle on because we believe that we can make a difference, that our contribution, however small, can bring the vision of a society in which children are able to grow up free from racism and other social inequalities one step closer to reality. To keep going we all need to acknowledge our successes and emotional support from people who are on the same wavelength as ourselves. As Louise Derman-Sparks (1993:28) says:

> Remember, by not acting we remain invisible and if we're invisible other people don't know that we exist either. We have to keep breaking down this sense of aloneness and invisibility. ... This work is hard but it is also very satisfying because of what we are trying to do in the process of this hard work. I think we also heal from the hurt that racism and the other isms inflict on us. So I think it is a wonderful way to be. There are times when we feel discouraged,

when we see all the obstacles but we need to get better at looking at our small victories, to be able to honour and celebrate them even though they are small and do not constitute the whole picture.

**Note**: I am using the term **educators** throughout the book to describe everyone who is concerned about the care and education of young children, e.g. childminders, playgroup workers, nursery nurses, teachers, welfare assistants, tutors, lecturers and residential care workers.

**Nursery/school** is used to cover all the services that cater for young children, e.g. playgroups, day nurseries, nursery schools.

**Parent(s)** is used to refer to adults responsible for the caring and rearing of young children, e.g. biological and adoptive parents, grandparents, foster parents.

**Black children and parents** includes those in mixed parentage families.

# Chapter 1
# Not too young to learn

*No one is born hating another person because of the colour of his skin, or his background or his religion. People must learn to hate, and if they can learn to hate, they can be taught to love, for love comes more naturally to the human heart than its opposite.* Nelson Mandela at his Inauguration as President of South Africa, 1994.

The main argument in this chapter is that while learning about the world around them children pick up both positive and negative attitudes and behaviour. Whether they live in small villages with only White adults and children, in middle class suburbs or in run-down inner city housing estates they are influenced by racism and other forms of discrimination. It does not seem to matter whether they have personal contact with Black and mixed parentage families, Traveller or refugee families or families in which adults or children are disabled. We can help them unlearn the misconceptions and stereotypical thinking they have absorbed.

Scientists have not been able to prove that attitudes are determined by genes. A reasonable assumption therefore seems to be that the environment, the people in it and the children themselves play a formative and crucial part. In the same way as young children learn attitudes to, for example, animals, books, food, they also learn racist and other discriminatory attitudes. They absorb a huge number of positive messages and also pick up mis-information, stereotypes, discriminatory attitudes and behaviour towards certain groups. During the first few years of life parents are usually the main role models for children and so it is not surprising that as they become aware of their parents' attitudes and values they reproduce them as their own. Their attitude formation is influenced also by other family and community members, books and toys, television programmes and advertisements. Although attitudes and values are transmitted consciously and unconsciously through direct and indirect teaching and role-learning, children do not simply absorb everything their parents, educators and peers tell them. There are many contradictory attitudes and ideologies within society that influence them. Troyna and Hatcher (1992) explored how children become socialised and warned against regarding them as empty slates. They believe that children choose how to make sense of their worlds – not all children of prejudiced parents share their parents' attitudes, beliefs and values.

## Learning begins

It is amazing how quickly and efficiently babies and young children are able to soak up and interpret information from the world around them. Even tiny babies are influenced by their surroundings and by the attitudes and behaviour of those who care for them but what babies learn and how they learn it depends on their experiences. Research published by the Carnegie Corporation (1994) highlights the importance of the first two years of life when the development of connections between brain cells depends on whether children receive appropriate stimulation. When they do, these vital connections are made and children's ability to learn and think become well grounded.

From babyhood, children are astute observers of the people around them even though they may be unable to conceptualise what they are observing or to pass value judgements. Through body language and gesture they become not only expert in conveying their needs and feelings but also very good at picking up feelings that adults may convey, whether consciously or unconsciously. From the way that people react to them they learn which of their actions are acceptable and which are not. Toddlers realise that they can make other children cry if they tease them and that if they comfort other children, they cry less. Dunn (1988) argues that they are aware of the feelings of others, they can comfort those who are distressed, they know how to annoy and upset others and to justify themselves. A three year old, for example, used stereotyped gender roles to justify her refusal to let her brother play with her toy vacuum cleaner. It seems reasonable to assume that when they are in group care children are learning about group living, about co-operation, social responsibility, awareness of others, empathy and acceptance.

As they grow and develop children pick up more and more verbal and non-verbal messages from adults, other children, the media and the general way society is organised. They absorb these messages whether or not they have personal contact with or knowledge about particular groups but the degree to which they are influenced depends, for example, on whether they are boys or girls, Black or White, abled or disabled, from middle class or working class families, from hetero-sexual or homosexual families, from Traveller or settled communities or if they are refugees. Their own personalities and experiences will also affect what they absorb, as will positive opportunities they have to counter this learning. However, it is important to stress that although the degree, extent and effect varies, the attitudes of all children are being and will continue to be affected as long as discriminatory atti-tudes and practices prevail in the wider society.

Studies like that of David Milner (1983) confirm that between three and five years old, British children learn to attach value to skin colour; they learn that there is a pecking order which places White at the top of the hierarchy and Black at the bottom. The message received by Black children is that society often sees them as outsiders, as inferior and of little significance. White children also make this evaluation be-cause they are growing up in a society which socialises them into thinking in racist stereotypes, into believing that they are physically, mentally and culturally superior.

While absorbing racist beliefs and ways of behaving, boys and girls are also picking up sexist attitudes and practices from the world around them. Weinraub and others (1984) claim that by around aged two they associate certain tasks and possessions such as cars and tools with men and vacuum cleaners and food with women. Many boys prefer to behave in ways that are traditionally associated with the male role and reject qualities that they have learnt to associate with the female role. Girls, on the other hand, behave in ways associated with both roles but see male roles as being more interesting and exciting. Helen Bee (1992:393) suggests that:

> An interesting sidelight in the research on stereotyping is that the male stereotype and sex-role concept seems to develop a bit earlier and to be stronger than the female stereotype or sex-role concept. More children agree on what men are or should be like than on what women are or should be ... At any rate, it is clear that the qualities attributed to the male are more highly valued than are female traits.

Between the ages of three and six, most children have developed a deeper understanding of themselves and their world. They are curious about differences and begin using prevailing negative stereotypes about people, including themselves, to express their thoughts and guide their actions. They may tease or refuse to play with children whose skin colour is darker than theirs, who speak languages different from theirs, dress differently or who have physical disabilities. They are learning what is the 'right' way to be a boy or a girl, what it means to be disabled, and what families are all about.

> Wendy, age three, informs her mother who is trying to dress her, 'Me not wearing trousers, me not a boy.'
>
> Tanya at three and a half refuses to sit next to dark-skinned Pamela.
>
> Five year old Ben argues with his friend Christopher that he can't have two mothers because, 'My dad told me that it's not allowed.'
>
> Five and a half year old Julie uses a wheelchair. Aubrey who is four won't play with her because he says, 'She's a baby in a pram and I don't play with babies.'

If children feel comfortable about talking about similarities and differences between people not only will they be more likely to ask lots of questions about why people are different but they will also provide their own reasons.

> 'People get to be black because a black bee bites them when they are born' claims five year old Rosa.
>
> 'Will you buy lots of melons for me to eat so my skin can get darker?' asks five year-old Peter after his teacher had talked about melanin.

Many young children from heterosexual families have learnt from various sources such as their homes, their playmates, the media and perhaps from us that lesbian/gay lifestyles are unacceptable and they have also learnt the vocabulary of homophobia.

> Two five year old boys were standing on a rather high wall about to jump off. One suggested they hold hands while they did it. The other refused saying, 'No, I don't want to. I'm not a poof.'

An incident quoted by Patrick and Burke (1993:201) illustrates not only that children tease their peers from lesbian families but also the different reactions of those being teased:

> Tom was very open about his 'two Mums', and his classmates used his openness as a way of upsetting him. He was upset precisely because the word lesbian is recognised to be an insult, even though he was not ashamed of his 'two Mums'. In the end, Martin, a very popular child in the same class, intervened. His mother was also in a lesbian relationship, but he never talked about it, either to the other children or to the teachers. However, he must have felt implicated, because on this occasion when Tom had been made upset over the issue, he said loudly, 'There's nothing wrong with being a lesbian. My Mum's a lesbian.'

Young children can differentiate between rich and poor adults and children by the clothes they wear, the houses they live in and by their possessions, even though they might not understand the concepts of wealth and poverty. They are beginning to believe that it is 'better' to be rich than to be poor and are learning that ownership is a source of power and control.

> Miranda at five confided to her child minder that she felt very sorry for her four year old cousin Susan, 'She hasn't got nice dresses like me and she's got nowhere to play with her toys 'cos she lives in a flat. Her mum hasn't even got a car.'

> A distressed Tommy greeted his mum when she came to fetch him from infant school with the words, 'It's not fair. Ben and Wayne said my trainers are rubbish. They're not 'spensive like theirs.'

## Learning racism – a closer look

The following examples support Milner's argument that children are influenced by racism from an early age:

> A student was about to read a book to four year old Sunita. On seeing the picture on the cover, she said: 'I don't want that story.' When asked the reason she pointed to the picture and replied: 'Cos she's got a brown face.'

> The student questioned her about the colour of the faces of her Grandmother, Mum, Dad, brother and baby sister. She replied in a quiet voice. 'They're brown.' But when asked what colour her own face was, she turned away and didn't respond.

Cecile Wright (1991:29) recorded this dialogue between Charlene, a three year old Black girl and Tina a four year old White girl.

Charlene:   (Cuddling a black doll) This is my baby.

Tina:       I don't like it, it's funny. I like this one (holding a white doll), it's my favourite. I don't like this one (pointing to the black doll). Because you see I like Sarah, and I like white. You're my best friend though, you're brown.

Charlene:   I don't like that one (pointing to the white doll).

Tina:       You're brown aren't you?

Charlene:   I'm not brown, I'm black.

Tina:       You're brown, but I'm white.

Charlene:   No I'm not, I'm black and baby's black.

Tina:       They call us white, my mummy calls me white, and you know my mummy calls you brown. When you come to visit, if you want ... She'll say 'hello brown person ...' I like brown, not black. Michael Jackson was brown, he went a bit white.

Chris Gaine (1992:9/10) cites some examples reported to him by his students while on teaching practice. He stresses that the children involved could not have picked up their ideas from first hand contact with the people they were disparaging and must have absorbed attitudes from the White community in which they were living:

> A student on her first teaching practice to a school in which all the children and staff were White, reported that as she entered the classroom one of the seven year olds exclaimed,: 'Oh God, it's a wog.'

> Another student used a selection of cards some produced by Save the Children that portrayed Jesus, Mary and Joseph with dark skins. The children were 7/8 year olds in Norfolk. Much to the student's surprise, because it wasn't what he was looking at, the children expressed negative views such as, 'I dislike the way that the Pakis are taking over everything, even Christmas.'

The observation below was written by a Nursery Nurse student on placement in an infant school in North London. She was upset because the teacher had described mothers in terms of their prettiness and was concerned about the reaction of one of the boys:

> The teacher talking to her reception class about Mother's Day showed them a picture of a woman and asked if they thought she was pretty. They all nodded in agreement. She then asked them to put up their hands if they thought that their mothers were pretty.

> All hands shot into the air. One little boy didn't respond.

> 'Don't you think that your Mummy is pretty?'

> 'No' he replied.

> 'Why don't you think that your Mummy is pretty?'

> 'Because she's brown.'

> The teacher then enquired whether he thought the lady in the picture was pretty.

> 'Yes, because she's white.'

## Learning sexism – a closer look

Davenport (1988:283) cites the work of Goldberg and Lewis, who found that six month old baby girls were likely to be held for longer periods and that their parents tended to speak to them in a softer tone of voice whereas the boys were treated and spoken to more robustly. Fagot's study, also quoted by Davenport (1988:283), looked at babies aged between twenty and twenty four months. Girl toddlers were encouraged to ask for help when they needed it, follow and stay near to a parent, dance, take an interest in girls' clothes for dressing up, play with dolls. They were discouraged from running around, jumping, climbing and generally being too active, being aggressive, playing 'rough' games, manipulating and exploring objects. Boys on the other hand were encouraged to play and explore toys such as trucks, building blocks, and things which encouraged strength and muscle building. They were discouraged from playing with dolls, asking for assistance, and anything thought to be 'feminine'.

By age five, children begin to associate certain personality traits with males or females. John Williams and Deborah Best (1990) found in their cross cultural study that the most clearly stereotyped traits for women were weakness, gentleness, appreciativeness and soft-heartedness while aggression, strength, cruelty and coarseness were identified for males. Interestingly, these traits were the most clearly stereotyped in virtually all of the twenty four countries surveyed.

Racist and sexist thinking and practices are closely tied up with one another and as children tend to learn them as a 'package', their attitudes to themselves, to others and to learning can be seriously affected. Connolly (1994) observed and interviewed five to six year olds in three parallel vertically grouped Reception/Year One classes. His findings suggest that they had learned that to be real boys they had to be competent at all sports, especially football. In competitive and public situations they often felt disappointed, frustrated and even angry. If they felt they had lost face White boys resorted to racist name-calling.

Work by Diane Reay (1993:15) with six year olds in a predominantly White middle class school highlights the consequences when boys learn that part of being 'macho' involves rejecting academic learning. Of eight disruptive and disaffected boys, four were working class and of these two were Black. They resisted the imposition of academic values, challenged the authority of women teachers and frequently opted out of learning. Reading and writing were regarded as 'feminine' activities because they did not fit in with the boys macho image of themselves. The only time that they remained on task was when they were working in small groups with a great deal of teacher attention which, Reay says, raises a question to which she has no answer. How far should we be devoting our energies to boys who already demand a disproportionate amount of time and attention at the expense of girls? She describes an exchange between herself and two of the boys:

> Steven was meticulously illustrating his book review. I praised the drawing, but pointed out that he was supposed to be writing. Steven ignored me and whispered something to Mark sitting next to him. Mark looked up at me and said, 'Steven doesn't like you.'
>
> I replied, 'That's alright, we can't like everybody.'
>
> A few seconds later, I tried again. 'Very good, Steven, now it's time to write. Which part of the story did you like the most?' Steven mumbled inaudibly and reluctantly started to write.
>
> A few minutes later, Mark tugged at my sleeve, 'Steven doesn't like you at all.' I couldn't resist a moralism, 'Well, I always wait until I know someone a bit better before I make up my mind about them!'
>
> Further whispers ensued, then Mark turned to me and delivered Steven's *coup de grace.* 'Steven says you're 35-40, you're a woman, you're a teacher, that's all he needs to know.'

Glenda MacNaughton (1995:1) observed and also recorded on video children playing in an Australian nursery school. She concluded that through their play boys and girls demonstrate that they have learned what is considered the proper and desirable way to be a boy or a girl and to be Black or White.

> In a nursery school Brian and Rachid, both aged five, were building a garage with bricks. Brian used gestures and language to tell Rachid where to place the bricks. Rachid placed each as directed.
>
> A five year old Vietnamese girl, Soon Lee, approached them and asked if she could play too. Brian lifted a brick and waved it in the air and shouted: 'No bloody wog girls here!'

Rachid imitated Brian's actions and words.

Soon Lee ran off crying to the teacher.

MacNaughton suggests that this incident provides important insights into the different ways in which gender and ethnicity influence play and are influenced by it. She believes that Rashid wanting to play with Brian and being racially-biased towards Soon Lee derived from his desire to get being a boy in Australia 'right'. Brian led, but Rachid also experienced power when, backing up Brian, he helped to exclude Soon Lee from the play. Their behaviour showed that they had learnt that to be a boy means yelling and threatening girls and not letting them play. Soon Lee was learning that being excluded was related to both her gender and her ethnicity.

MacNaughton (1995:15) also observed Natalie, Tanya, and Shelley in the home corner and recorded their play on video. These three girls, all nearly five, spent a considerable part of their day involved in domestic play. The fact that Natalie and Tanya were Black and that Shelley was White had been seen by the teacher as a positive development. However, close observation of their play revealed the unequal power relationships between them. Certain roles, for example that of mum in domestic play, give children power. Natalie and Tanya made various attempts to be 'mum' but were always firmly told by Shelley that *she* was 'mum' and that they were the babies, whom she proceeded to tell what to do and when to do it. She experienced a strong sense of power as she dictated, in a commanding tone of voice, the storyline they were to follow, e.g. preparing for a party, watching TV or feeding baby. This was how the play unfolded during one of the five observations MacNaughton recorded:

Shelley to Tanya:     You can be sister, big sister. Put the baby to sleep, sleepy sleep.

Tanya goes to the doll's beds and picks up a black doll.

Shelley to Tanya:     No, not that way, you always play with that one, no the other baby (points to a white doll).

Tanya hesitates but then obeys and picks up a white doll. The play continues for a while with the three busily preparing lunch for the baby and sisters. Shelley rushes to the toilet. Tanya picks up the black doll and starts feeding it but has put it back down before Shelley returns.

In none of the five observations was Shelley overtly personally racist towards her friends, i.e. she did not exclude or directly demean either Natalie or Tanya and the play seemed harmonious. However, on closer analysis, racially and sexually biased relationships were evident in Shelley's disapproval and devaluing of the black doll – of which Tanya was clearly aware – and the exclusion of both Natalie and Tanya from being 'mum'. MacNaughton believes that Natalie and Tanya stayed in the game and did nothing to challenge Shelley's power overtly because they considered domestic play to be the normal and desirable activity for girls. They gained considerable pleasure because they were getting the task of being a girl 'right'. They had learned that the right way to be a girl was to involve themselves in traditional gender-appropriate activities like playing with dolls and dressing as 'proper little girls'. Being subservient to boys, non-aggressive and avoiding confrontation at all costs are also part of what being a girl is all about. Boys have learned that the way to be a boy is to play with 'boy's toys', be aggressive and be anti-girl.

MacNaughton proposes that the sexist and racist power relationships that she observed in the play of Australian children also characterises play in other societies where sexist and racist relationships are woven into the fabric, such as in the United States and Britain. Closely observing and assessing the extent to which play is discriminatory can help us decide how and when to intervene to counter the stereotypical thinking children have already learned and build relationships that are based on anti-discriminatory understandings.

## What is learned can be unlearned

Children absorb misconceptions from the discriminatory actions and stereotypical attitudes they see and hear, as well as from the way adults respond to their observations and questions about differences in skin colour and physical features – as happened in the following incident:

A four year old White child travelling in a bus says in a loud voice: 'Look at that brown lady over there.'

Everyone freezes with embarrassment and the flustered mother tells her: 'That's not a nice thing to say.'

She desperately distracts the child who is left with the feeling that being brown is not nice and shouldn't be talked about.

The key worker in the following incident lost an opportunity to provide children with appropriate information to counter their misconceptions.

Jo, a three year old of an African-Caribbean background, was adopted by White parents. He has a White brother and is the only Black child in the day nursery. On this particular day four children including Jo were looking at some photos. One of them pointing, to a group of Black children, said: 'Look, there's your brothers and sisters, Jo.'

'Oh yes,' they all readily agreed, except Jo who looked bewildered and upset.

His key worker asked, 'Why do you think those children are Jo's brothers and sisters?'

The children looking puzzled and embarrassed, said nothing. They had recognised that Jo was a Black child and felt uncomfortable when questioned. Jo, on the other hand, was left not understanding why the children referred to complete strangers as his brothers and sisters. By not encouraging the children to talk about their reaction, the key worker probably increased their confusion and their store of misinformation.

Young children also seem to pick up unspoken messages that there are times and situations when they are expected to express what they feel and others when they should not. The study by Jeffcoate (1979:13) shows that White children may learn that it's not a good idea to express negative attitudes in front of adults:

The head teacher in an all White nursery school in Bradford invited four year old children to talk about non-stereotypical pictures of Black and White people doing a variety of jobs. As they made no reference to skin colour during the ensuing discussion the head teacher's contention that young children do not discriminate between people on the basis of the colour of their skin was confirmed. However, in the afternoon when the same set of pictures were left on the tables without any input from the head teacher, the children responded differently. Not only did they refer to skin colour but their increasingly negative and derisory comments forced the head teacher to step in and end the session.

If children's perceptions of people who are different from themselves are based on stereotypical thinking it is likely that they will retain this misinformation for the rest of their lives unless positive steps are taken to counter this learning. Some of the stereotypes that they have absorbed are so deeply ingrained that they have become part of the English language. The fact that children may never have had any personal experience of the group they are stereotyping does not affect the ease with which the stereotypes are accepted or the way they trip lightly off their tongues. The following incident took place while two eight year olds, Mary and Jean, were working on the computer in the school library:

> Mary asked Jean to lend her 10p so that she could buy some crisps. Jean refused. Mary retorted, 'Oh you mean f........ Jew. Stop jewing me.'
>
> The librarian intervened. 'What was that you said?'
>
> Mary stammered, 'Oh sorry Miss! I didn't see you there. Don't tell I said that'.
>
> 'Said what?' the librarian asked.
>
> 'The 'F' word' was the reply.
>
> 'Do you know any Jews?' the librarian asked.
>
> 'No' they both said.

Although neither child had any personal contact with Jewish people, they had learned the stereotype of Jewish people as being mean. To both of them, to be mean was to be a Jew. Mary didn't have to explain to Jean what she meant by, 'Stop jewing me' – they both understood.

The next example illustrates that, given the appropriate input and encouragement, children can, and do, unlearn misconceptions and stereotypes.

> One morning a Nursery worker, Pauline, and a group of Black and White boys and girls aged between three and four were enjoying story time. At the end of the session the Nursery worker asked them what they would like to do next.

| | |
|---|---|
| Emily: | Let's play Cinderella. |
| Pauline: | That's a good idea. Can I be Cinderella? |
| Emily: | No you can't. |
| Pauline: | Why not? |
| Emily: | Because you're Black. |
| Pauline: | Why can't I be Cinderella because I'm Black? |
| Emily: | 'Cause Cinderella is White in my storybook and on my video. |

Emily had made a judgement based on the limited information available to her. During the discussion that followed Pauline acknowledged that Emily was right – all the Cinderellas she had ever seen were White. But she then helped Emily and the other children to realise that Cinderella and all the other characters in the story could as easily be Black as White. Pauline encouraged them to look at and talk about the illustrations in other books in the nursery. The fact that management and staff were committed to working from an antiracist perspective ensured that the books included positive images of Black people in a wide range of stories and the children were accustomed to stories in which the main character was Black. A member of staff suggested that Pauline follow this incident by reading the book, *Amazing Grace* by Mary Hoffman, about a little Black girl who is told by her friends that she can't play the part of Peter Pan in the forthcoming play because she is a girl and because she is Black. Feeling very hurt and upset, Grace talks it over with her Granny, who tells her that she can do anything she wants to do. At the audition, all her friends think that she's the best and she gets the part. The children loved the story and talked about their feelings and about the things they had done, what they could do and what they had achieved. Practice like this illustrates how an anti-discriminatory approach in the early years provides a foundation on which children's future learning can be built. A culturally appropriate curriculum can ensure that all children and their families feel included, valued, motivated and empowered. By countering the misinformation and stereotypical thinking that they have already learned, we contribute to the all-round development of children.

Chapter 2

# Anti-Discriminatory Practice is Good Educational Practice

*Everybody has the capacity to change but some people die before they do*. Louise Derman-Sparks

This chapter considers the influence of discriminatory attitudes on education policy and practice. How are children's attitudes to learning, self-esteem, expectations of other children and their own aspirations and performance affected by society's stereotyping and labelling? Arguments are put forward to explain why a compensatory approach is discriminatory and why multicultural education on its own fails to counter racism. It is proposed that to be effective multiculturalism needs to be part and parcel of an antiracist approach. The chapter ends by identifying the factors that need to be considered when implementing anti-discriminatory practice.

Up until 1870 the British education system, as in many other countries, was accessible mainly to children whose families had the money to pay for it. Gradually the doors were opened wider and today all children have the right, and are in fact compelled by law, to receive an education. Although it is generally agreed that the education system should provide equality of opportunity, it disproportionately allocates success to middle class, White, able-bodied boys and girls. This is not surprising considering its history, the way it is organised and how and what is taught. For example, much of what we adults were taught when we were at school and what children learn today fails to include information like the following:

- Florence Nightingale and Mary Seacole, a Black woman, contributed to nursing during the Crimean War.

- Harriet Tubman, a Black slave in America, set up the 'Underground Railroad' through which over 300 slaves escaped to Canada.

- Nanny, the Maroon leader, defied her brother Cudjoe and the British in her mountain stronghold until betrayed into surrendering.

- Sojourner Truth was the first African-American anti-slavery lecturer, abolitionist and crusader for women's rights. A well-known activist, she was the only person speaking out at the time for those oppressed by racism and sexism.

- Traffic lights were invented by a Black man, Garrett Morgan, and a Black doctor, Charles Drew, developed the technique of storing blood that made transfusions possible and performed the first heart surgery.

- While humanitarians fought hard for the abolition of slavery, it was the uprisings and escapes by the slaves themselves which made the system economically unviable and led to its abolition.

- India had her own thriving cotton industry before becoming part of the British Empire. It was then systematically dismantled to avoid competition with the cotton mills in Lancashire.

- In the 1500s Timbuktu in central West Africa was a city of scholars and learning.

- Some very 'British' games like Snakes and Ladders and Ludo originated in India.

The ways in which problems are defined and the solutions that have been proposed over the years continue to be strongly influenced by stereotypical thinking and by the conscious or unconscious perception that White middle class values, beliefs and lifestyles are superior to others. Educational policies and the thinking on which they are based evolve and change, though the attitudes that informed previous policies and practice continue to affect present ones. For example, discredited theories put forward by Jensen (1969) and Eysenck (1971) which explained Black children's under-achievement in terms of their genetically different and inferior intelligence still tend to influence current thinking.

## Give a dog a bad name

As we all know, children are powerfully affected by the attitudes, values and beliefs of adults. Encouragement, praise and realistic levels of expectation all act as a spur. Rosenthal and Jacobsen (1968) showed that children tend to live up to teachers' expectations of them and that these can have long term effects on their motivation to learn and their self-esteem. If expectations are high, children 'bloom'. Purkey (1970) correlated high self-esteem with high academic performance and Lawrence (1988) showed that children's self-esteem is influenced by their perception of how others accept them and see them as competent and worthwhile.

Some highly able children become aggressive or disinterested if too little is expected of them. On the other hand it is possible that the relatively high incidence of suicide and mental breakdown among university students is in part due to their having been exposed from early childhood to expectations that they felt they couldn't live up to and which put them under constant pressure. Conversely, expectations pitched at too low a level cause children to adopt a correspondingly low standard of effort and achievement. When we are interacting with children of whom we have low expectations we tend to demand less work, wait less time for answers, criticise more and praise less, spend less time with them and give less feedback.

A small number of children adopt the attitude, 'I'll show them I'm not stupid' and try as hard as they can to prove their educators wrong. But this is not, unfortunately, the general rule.

If expectations of children from particular groups are based on negative stereotypes, they could be labelled as non-achievers and therefore not expected to achieve. Thus educators set up a self-fulfilling prophecy – they get the results they expected. The children pick up subtle and overt messages that they are not expected to succeed intellectually and they behave accordingly. The Swann Report (1985:420) quotes from the evidence presented by the National Association for the Teaching of English:

> Teachers often expect that children who speak languages or dialects different from their own will have grave difficulties. Research has shown that it is the teachers' expectation, not the different dialect that causes the difficulties.

The process through which children live down to, confirm and reinforce our expectations occurs in a spiral. The impact may not be immediately evident, but because young children are very sensitive, their subsequent approach to learning can be negatively affected. Iram Siraj-Blatchford (1995:44)) however, claims that the perceptions that children have of themselves affects their attitudes and actions:

> ... we might find in our classrooms black and other ethnic minority children who are very academically successful in spite of the structural, cultural and interpersonal racism in our society. Similarly, we will find working class boys who are caring and unaggressive and African Caribbean boys who are able and well-behaved. The sexism, racism and other inequalities in our society can explain why at a structural level certain groups of people have less power while others have more. But at the level of agency we should beware of stereotypes and focus on individual people.

A stereotype is an over-simplified generalisation not based on evidence and which usually carries negative implications. For example, it is a fact that women are biologically different from men but there is no evidence to back the common stereotype that they are intellectually inferior. Irish people do not all behave in the same way, nor do English people or French or any other group of people. Stereotyping carries serious consequences including inaccurate judgements, inappropriate expectations, prejudiced assumptions, unsatisfactory personal relationships, unfairness and inequality. People on the receiving end usually feel angry, frustrated, alienated, hurt, ashamed, humiliated and insulted. One response is for adults and children to internalise these negative beliefs, i.e. to believe that these misconceptions are in fact true and that they apply to themselves. On the other hand, they might respond by withdrawing or behaving aggressively.

Black children growing up in a racist society and receiving verbal and non-verbal messages that they are less valued and that less is expected from them may not be motivated to learn. If they are constantly being presented with a 'White' world, they may find it more difficult to develop a sense of identity and feelings of personal worth. The pride and sense of belonging which they draw from their families and communities will limit the extent of the damage but, like all children, if they are not encouraged, valued, praised and expected to achieve, they may give up and stop trying. Jim Cummins (1996) argues that many Black children withdraw academically because the messages they receive devalue their identity and that these messages are the same ones as their parents received when they were children.

## How racist stereotyping influences expectations of Black children

Racial stereotypes have roots deeply embedded in British history. During the time Britain was the world's leading slave trader, the notion evolved that black people were naturally inferior, less advanced, less virtuous so it was alright for 'us' to buy and sell 'them'. Later, when the British Empire dominated and exploited vast areas and peoples of the world, these views were reinforced. The assumption was that English traditions and life-style are the 'right ones' and that others were not quite as 'good'. These views still continue to influence many White educators' expectations of Black children. Books widely used on child-care courses in the 1970s and 1980s unwittingly reinforced such stereotypical assumptions. These extracts appeared in the second edition, (but not in later ones), of a book by Brain and Martin (1983:45):

> West Indian children may appear to have a 'different' emotional make-up, and will cry and fight, laugh and love with equal energy. Their responsiveness to music makes it almost impossible for them to remain still when music is played. Many Asian families are from rural areas, and the noise and bustle of the nursery may be overwhelming. The children may be missing the stimulation and companionship of village life and the extended family, now that in

England the mother goes to work. Asian children may appear very passive and dependent on adults, as they are encouraged to be dependent and obedient in their families. Young Chinese children may be involved in the family business if there is one, because this is their culture – that *all* contribute to the family income. If the business is catering, hours may not be compatible with ideal children's bedtimes, and in the nursery the children may appear fatigued. Children are encouraged in the home to be docile and hard-working. Education is rated very highly. The children are often intelligent and learn quickly. They are usually quiet, extremely polite and well-behaved.

Accepting these stereotypical assessments have led educators and students to expect all Chinese children to be high achievers, all Asian children to be submissive and lacking initiative and all African-Caribbean children to be very physical and exuberant. Perhaps it is not surprising that the Ofsted Report (1996) notes that teachers still tend to accept the stereotypical assumption that Asian children are quiet, well behaved and highly motivated.

Large numbers of Black parents believe that their children fail to achieve their full academic potential because White educators have a stereotypical view of Black children, especially boys, as having physical rather than intellectual abilities and so find concentrating difficult. African-Caribbean parents report that educators let their boys spend every day tearing around on bicycles or just running about instead of encouraging them to participate in stimulating creative activities or to complete challenging puzzles. They claim that in nurseries/schools where teachers have high expectations of their children, they do well.

In her participant study Cecile Wright (1991) found that many White staff expected bad behaviour, especially from the African-Caribbean boys. They were frequently reprimanded, excluded from class, sent to the headteacher, or had their privileges withdrawn. From conversations in the staff room it appeared that being subject to negative expectations and labelled as 'very disruptive' dated back to when the African-Caribbean boys and Rastafarian children were in the nursery class. The teachers' logs in which they recorded daily experiences suggest that some expressed their frustration by negatively stereotyping and insulting the African-Caribbean children. This example recorded by Wright (1991:28) refers to Justin, a six year old African-Caribbean boy:

> ... I've seldom seen a face like it on a child. The temper, rage and marked aggression was quite frightening to see. I wouldn't be surprised in years to come if Justin wasn't capable of actually killing someone. When he smiles he could charm the birds off the trees, but when he's in a temper he is incapable of controlling himself. He has an extremely short fuse, is a real chauvinist and to cap it all he's got a persecution complex. He has to be handled with kid gloves.

It is quite possible that attitudes identified in this research contribute to the disproportionate number of African-Caribbean children being referred to units for children who have serious emotional and behavioural problems, or being suspended or excluded. Reports point to the fact that a disproportionate number of Black boys, especially those from African-Caribbean backgrounds, are being excluded. For example, evidence gathered during Ofsted inspections (1993/94) show that Black boys are six to eight times more likely to be excluded than other children. Black girls are also over-represented in the figures but not to the same extent, although the rate is increasing. Figures like these are disturbing, especially as younger children are being excluded, even at five or six.

Wright also found that although Asian children were not thought of as badly behaved, they were nevertheless considered to be problems. Their cultural background tended to be viewed negatively and they were generally considered to have poor language skills. When teasing and harassing the Asian children, White children would play on the very features to which the teachers had drawn attention in the classroom.

Black educators often have greater aspirations for and expectations of Black children than their White colleagues. Annan (1993:99) who is Black and teaching in a primary school in North London puts it this way:

> I feel that I inevitably have a greater insight into the difficulties black children may encounter, either because of the colour of their skin or their culture. Because of this I attempt to give a high profile

to race issues. In practice this means, first and foremost, attempting to ensure children fulfill their potential by having consistently high expectations of them, as well as helping to develop positive self-images and trying to tackle racist behaviour in a constructive way.

## How stereotyping influences expectations of Irish, Greek and Turkish Cypriot children

Negative stereotypes that evolved to justify the colonisation and continuing British rule in Northern Ireland brand Irish people as wild, stupid, drunken and inherently violent. These stereotypes are expressed in attitudes and behaviour, Irish 'jokes' and negative portrayal in the media. If as educators we have unconsciously absorbed these stereotypes we could have low expectations of Irish children. If we do not expect Irish children to achieve we are likely to reinforce negative attitudes towards Irish people that other children in the group may already have picked up. Children tend to be sharply aware of how we label their peers.

The following conversation took place in a staff room. What particularly upset the student who recorded it was that assumptions like these were so often expressed:

Ms Rose:    Did you see the way that Patrick behaved again during Assembly this morning? I really don't know what to do with him. He's as thick as two planks and so aggressive. He hits out at the slightest provocation.

Ms. Penn:    He certainly is a handful. But it's not really surprising when you look at his parents. I wouldn't be the least bit surprised if they spend every night in the pub with their cronies.

Ms Rose:    And I bet they leave all those children on their own. No sense of responsibility.

The Swann Report (1985:16) claims that the tendency to view people from other countries as 'inferior' is a legacy of history:

Youngsters from the Greek Cypriot community were generally seen very much in a positive light as enriching the cultural wealth of the classroom whilst those from the Turkish Cypriot community tended to be viewed negatively as potential underachievers and disruptive elements. In discussions with representatives of both communities there was general agreement that the causes for this surprising variation lay firstly in the difference in skin colour – Greek Cypriot children tending to be lighter skinned than their Turkish Cypriot peers, this seemingly being equated, in the minds of some teachers, with greater academic ability – and secondly in the very different historical stereotypes which exist of the Greeks and the Turks – the former being seen as a major influence on the evolution of Western civilisation and culture, and the latter as 'barbarians'.

## How gender stereotyping influences expectations of girls and boys

The ideas we hold of what is right and proper for girls and for boys also influence the way we speak and behave towards children and our expectations of them as these typical comments from a student on a nursery nursing course indicate:

Greg is a real boy, always active and up to mischief but Sydney's different, he's shy and he clings to Nadia. He's a real mother's boy. Andrew, Sean and Tony are so naughty and boisterous but Deborah is very loving and helpful – a sweet little girl.

However children are active participants in the learning process and do not necessarily do what is expected of them! A mother complains: '*Jane never plays with dolls. I bought her a lovely doll last Christmas but she never touches it. She just likes to be outside riding around as fast as she can on her tricycle*'.

Nevertheless, differences in the expectations and treatment of boys and girls frequently cause them to accept a stereotypical view of themselves and their place in society and influence their response to learning. If we let girls spend the greater part of the day in domestic and quiet areas rather than steering them towards construction toys and problem-solving activities we fail to develop their interest in and ability to do mathematics and science later on. However, the requirements of the National Curriculum are influencing the expectations and performance of girls by placing a responsibility on educators to ensure that both boys and girls are encouraged to develop their knowledge and ability in *all* subjects. While girls have shown a marked improvement in Science and Technology, boys continue to underachieve in reading and writing. The pressure on them to be strong and tough leads some boys to turn their backs on all 'intellectual' activities and so negatively affects their progress at school.

To break down stereotypes, widen girls' future aspirations and foster their curiosity about how things work, we could set up tinkering tables with screwdrivers, spanners and things to take apart like old clocks and telephones. To try and break down the 'macho' attitude of boys we might encourage them to become involved in quiet, but challenging and stimulating intellectual activities. Close observation of children can help to change stereotypical assumptions, as this Nursery Nurse student on placement managed to do:

> Her parents and her key worker described three year old Margaret as a 'typical' girl. She spent the morning playing quietly 'in her own little world' and was not expected or encouraged to explore other options. However, while observing her, a student on placement noticed that she didn't seem to be able to listen to stories or want to communicate with the other children but that when they did talk to her, she concentrated on their faces with a pained expression on hers. Having watched her over a number of days, the student suggested that perhaps she had a hearing impairment. Careful observation and a hearing test revealed this to be the case. Medical intervention solved the problem. Instead of perpetuating the gender stereotype, the key worker changed her approach and her expectations of Margaret, who began to take an active interest in the life of the nursery.

## How stereotyping influences expectations of children from Traveller families

If we subscribe to the stereotype of Travellers as dirty, thieving, unreliable, irresponsible and stupid, our expectations of children from these families will be low and we will view their lifestyle negatively. We may not appreciate that the children are likely to have a fund of practical knowledge – such as how long a litre of petrol lasts in a generator – understand the concept of distance, have first-hand experience of plants and animals. There are, of course, educators who welcome Traveller children, where, in the words of one twelve year old girl: '*This school is different. Here they expect you to learn. The others expect you to move on.*'

The Swann Report (1985:756) came to this conclusion on Traveller education:

> In many ways the situation of Traveller children in Britain today throws into stark relief many of the factors which influence the education of children from other ethnic minority groups – racism and discrimination, myths, stereotyping, misinformation, the in-appropriateness and inflexibility of the education system and the need for better links between homes and schools and teachers and parents. ... ways can and must be found to reconcile the concerns and aspirations of the travelling community and the mainstream education system in a much more positive manner.

The Ofsted Report (1996a) provides evidence of improving levels of achievement by many Traveller pupils, especially at Key Stage 1, but also considerable underachievement. It suggests that progress over the last ten years has been relatively slow because it is dependent on changing deep-rooted attitudes:

> The response to school of Travelling pupils is crucially influenced by the Travelling children's awareness of the level of their accep-tance by teachers and other pupils. Where the presence of Travel-ling children is openly acknowledged, and where accurate and positive resources of the different nomadic communities are featured within both the resources of the school and the curri-culum, then the response is lively and there is a genuine openness to learning. In contrast, where the ethos of the school implicitly or explicitly suggests that Travelling pupils are best served by an incognito status ... the response lacks confidence, is tentative and reserved. This situation can also lead to behaviour difficulties. Travelling pupils appear to achieve higher standards in schools which place great emphasis on equality of opportunity and by

encouraging the acceptance of cultural and ethnic diversity, establish an ethos which fosters self-esteem and pride in individual and group identity. Such a philosophy manifests itself through both the formal and informal curriculum ... Where this is done well it has helped to improve the quality of learning and accuracy of knowledge for all pupils.

## THROUGH THE EYES OF A CHILD

By Julie Gentle – an extract quoted by Etherington (1993)

The Travelling life was wonderful
Nothing to do but play
Until we moved onto a site
And you're starting school today
Don't put him next to me
My mam'll have a fit
They never have a wash
And I might catch a nit

Watch him try and write
He can't even spell his name
God, he is so stupid
Isn't it a shame

He's sitting drawing pictures
Of a horse and caravan
He says he's going to own one
When he becomes a man

He knows the price of metals
Scrap and woollens too
He can prune a tree and tarmac
Sell carpets, flowers too

The bell rings for a break
It's time to take a walk
The Gypsy stands alone
nobody wants to talk

A group of boys come over
Shouting names at him
Two or three catch hold of him
While the others kick his shin

When they let him go
Our Gypsy he hits out
Then the dinner lady
Runs over with a shout

Don't you hit our kids
You dirty Gyppo you
I'm taking you to a teacher
He'll know just what to do

They go down to the site
They want to see his Dad
We don't want him at our school
He's behaving very bad

So now you know why Gypsies
Don't bother with the schools.
Cause you end up the guilty ones
Being treated just like fools.

## Low expectations and disabled children

Many educators and parents of disabled children believe strongly that all children have the right to be included in mainstream nurseries/schools. The Fish Report, (1985) put forward a policy based on the view that physical disabilities and learning difficulties become more or less handicapping depending on the expectations of others. Integration offers benefits for children with special needs and for the other children in the group and is most successful in nurseries/schools in which educators enjoy working with children who have a range of abilities and do not over-protect them but respond to the challenge to encourage and expect them all to do as well as they can.

In Italy where they have been successfully integrating children since 1971, the classes are small and a good deal of support is available. In the competitive atmosphere of most British mainstream schools and where disabled children may lack self-esteem and confidence in their own abilities, their feelings of failure and inadequacy are likely to be reinforced if their educators do not expect them to succeed and they are in groups with large numbers of children.

Some parents, educators and disabled people are worried that integration is a thinly disguised strategy to save money. They argue that although standards vary in special schools, the experienced and specially trained teachers are more likely to be able to meet children's needs and to have more realistic expectations than their colleagues teaching in mainstream schools. Margaret Parrish (1997:13) believes that:

> Children who are born deaf use their dominant sense, sight, to learn about the world around them and they need the British Sign Language (BSL) to capitalise on that sense. Denying them access to sign language represents a blatant discrimination against deaf children. Teaching deaf children in special units with specialist teachers and using sign language ... provides adult role models, the mutual support of other deaf children and an awareness of the deaf community and its culture. ... But true integration for deaf children would mean they all had access to BSL and their own interpreter – and that would be far more costly than retaining special schools.

Those who support integration point out that educators in some special schools over-protect the children and expect very little from them. Integration, they argue, means that abled and disabled children can come together, adapt and accommodate each other's needs and learn new skills. Taylor and Costley (1995:21) suggest that:

> Having artificial, legally defined boundaries between the 'normal' and 'not normal' may lead to discriminatory thinking and practice. This deficit model of assessing individual needs ultimately compromises the goals of inclusive education. Rather than thinking of 'special needs', would it therefore not be more enabling to think of individual needs; recognising that from time to time every one of us has needs which require extra support, no matter what our physical or intellectual capacities?

## Failing children

In the 1950s and 1960s poor attainment by working class Black and White children was explained in terms of cultural deprivation and compensation. The 'problem' was that parents were not developing their children's intellectual capacity i.e. they were not giving them the 'right' kind of experiences or using the 'right' kind of language and so were depriving their children of the stimulation that their peers in middle class homes were receiving. Parents needed to change their cultural practices to enable their children to succeed. It was recommended that nurseries/schools set up compensatory education programmes to iron out the deficiencies that children were perceived to be experiencing at home. Douglas (1967) was among the sociologists who confirmed and highlighted the mismatch between the homes of working class children and their nurseries/schools and supported the compensatory education policy. The Plowden Report (1967) also affirmed these ideas. However, other researchers challenged the notions of cultural deprivation and compensatory education. Tizard and Hughes (1984) found that the language in the homes of all the children they studied tended to be richer than it was in nurseries/schools and that the differences between the language used by working and middle class families were very small. Ginsburg (1972) argued that although poverty is undesirable it does not retard people's ability to think and reason. Margy Whalley (1994) supports this view. She claims that poverty was being equated with cultural deprivation, that culture was being linked exclusively to middle class values and that many programmes misrepresented what parents were actually doing with their children at home and stereotyped them along class lines.

In addition to notions of cultural deprivation and compensation, a policy of assimilation was applied to education in the 1950s and 1960s. The belief was that Black adults and children coming to live in Britain ought to adopt 'British culture and way of life' in place of their own – that 'when in Rome, do as the Romans do.' Black children were expected to leave their culture at home when they came to nursery/school. Sandell (1993:16) remembers her experiences during her first week in a British infant school – over thirty years ago:

> I came to this country from Jamaica in 1960 just before I was eight. Because everyone there knew I would be coming here to join my parents, I had not been to school before. So my first experience of school was in Britain. What stood out in my mind in that first week was a teacher standing in front of the class encouraging us to sing about a little teapot. My eyes must have been the size of saucers because in Jamaica, children use two slang terms for parts of a boy's anatomy – one was 'teelis', the other 'teapot'. Here was this very wise person reciting it in front of the class, and gesticulating the action as well. The story is a funny one, but I was distressed, as sex was taboo for children in the culture I came from. My reaction – I ended up rushing out of the classroom in tears – led to a dressing down by the teacher. If I was going to adjust to the school, I had to behave like English people, I was told. ... It has taken a long time in my adult life to reintroduce myself to the Jamaican parts of myself.

## The multicultural approach

In the 1970s protests by Black parents who continued to feel that the education system was failing to meet the needs of their children helped to shift policy away from assimilation and compensation towards multiculturalism. The spotlight shifted from White working class children's lack of success to focus on Black children, especially on the boys. Black children were believed to have a poor self-image and this was considered to be the reason why they were not achieving. It was hoped that reflecting Black children's cultural practices in nurseries/ schools and providing them with opportunities to share aspects of their cultures with their peers would raise their self-esteem and so increase their chances to succeed academically. Official policy was summed up in the Rampton report (1981:27) which stated that:

> A 'good' education cannot be based on one culture only, and in Britain where ethnic minorities form a permanent and integral part of the population, we do not believe that education should seek to iron out the differences between cultures, nor attempt to draw everyone into the dominant culture. On the contrary, it will draw upon the experiences of the many cultures that make up our society and thus broaden the cultural horizons of every child. That is what we mean by 'multicultural education'.

It was also anticipated that encouraging White children to learn about other cultures would help them become less racially prejudiced. The belief that racism and racial conflict are caused by cultural ignorance and misunderstanding underpins the concept of multicultural education.

Nurseries/schools that adopted a multicultural approach introduced resources to reflect the home cultures of the children attending the nursery/school. Parents were invited to help with cooking sessions with the children, introducing dishes from their cultures. Multicultural evenings were organised to enable staff, parents and children to mix socially. Equal opportunities policies were formulated in nurseries/ schools and translation services provided by local authorities to ensure that notices in nurseries/schools and letters sent out were accessible to all the parents. Festivals were enthusiastically celebrated, including some that many of us had never heard of before.

In varying degrees most nurseries/schools today incorporate a range of cultural practices into the curriculum. By recognising the important role that culture plays in the lives of children, multicultural education represents a significant step forward. It has, however, been criticised on a number of grounds:

• As it was initially introduced into multiracial nurseries/schools and not into those in which all the children were White, many educators believed that multicultural education was for Black children. Some still do – this attitude continues to be expressed in comments such as, 'We don't need it, we've got none of them in our nursery/school' and, 'I don't see why my children who are all White have to learn about other cultures'. The Swann Report (1985:228) noted that:

> The concept of multicultural education being of relevance to all children, including those attending 'all white' schools, appears to have failed to impinge in practice on non-multiracial areas, which still seemingly equate multicultural education with the actual presence of ethnic minority pupils and therefore tend to explain their lack of concern with such developments by simply pointing out that they have no ethnic minority pupils.

• Multicultural education ignores the existence of unequal power relationships and the fact that racism is embedded in the fabric of British society. It fails to acknowledge the existence of the deeply rooted hierarchy of cultures that exists in Britain in which Black cultures are lowly ranked. Also unacknowledged is the fact that although White middle class culture is dominant and highly ranked, certain White cultures such as Irish and Jewish are less valued.

• A multicultural approach does not necessarily change children's negative views about, or attitudes towards, other cultures and lifestyles. Simply learning about cultures and appreciating cultural differences, the way other people do things and the way 'they' celebrate 'their' festivals has little impact on the negative attitudes children already hold towards adults and children from these cultures. An example quoted by Burgess-Macey and Crichlow (1996:76) makes this clear:

> A teacher had planned that the children would make and eat samosas. When a white child refused to take part in the activity because this was 'paki' food the teacher did not know how to respond and simply reprimanded the child, 'Don't be rude'. The child then departed for another activity leaving the teacher feeling uncomfortable and Asian children in the group feeling

upset, quite possibly wishing that the activity had been to make sandwiches.

Positive attempts to address multicultural issues can lead to ambivalent feelings. On the one hand, children may feel proud about having aspects of their traditions or customs acknowledged yet on the other this may precipitate more teasing, ridicule and harassment.

- Offering children a narrow multicultural curriculum which focuses on 'exotic' cultures does not create an atmosphere of respect in which children are valued and positive relationships are built with parents.

- Teaching the multicultural way involves giving children snapshot impressions of various cultures and runs the risk of encouraging crude stereotypes like 'All Chinese people eat with chopsticks, work hard and respect their elders'.

- A multicultural approach also fails to take account of what Black parents want for their children i.e. ensuring that they learn cognitive skills and, as one mother put it, 'We want children to learn to fight racism, not to tie a sari.' Many Black parents, especially those from the African-Caribbean community, feel that multicultural education stereotypes and interferes with their children's education because they are taken out of mainstream curricular activities to take part in dance and music events. Yet many educators argue that by involving them in activities in which they are successful, the children's self-esteem is being boosted.

- The focus of the multicultural approach tends to be on the cultures of Asian people from the Indian sub-continent and on people from the Caribbean. The presence of those whose cultural heritage stems from Africa, the rest of Asia, Latin America, or the Middle East, is generally trivialised or forgotten and the diverse cultural heritages of White children frequently unacknowledged. It is a focus that can lead to misunderstanding and conflict. The MacDonald Report (1989) into the murder of a pupil, Ahmed Iqbal Ullah, at a Manchester school for boys stressed that the staff inadvertently created resentment and fear among the White working class pupils. They felt that their own cultures and experiences were being devalued and marginalised by the (middle class) school while those of the ethnic minorities were being given priority treatment. Hewitt (1996) finds similar feelings about their own culture among white working-class people in Eltham.

- The final and perhaps most crucial argument is that the promotion of cultural diversity, religious tolerance and understanding between children of different 'races' and cultures is important but is insufficient on its own. Multiculturalism needs to be embedded in an anti-discriminatory framework so that racist attitudes and practices can be challenged. A good place to start is with young White children in whom power and authority are likely to be vested in the future.

## An anti-discriminatory approach

While they are growing up most children have painful memories of being treated unfairly and know what it feels like to be powerless, to be told in a 'no-nonsense' tone what they have to do and how to behave. Most have experienced being stereotyped because of their age, gender, class, ability, ethnic or regional origin, or the way they speak and they, in turn, have stereotyped others. We can encourage them to draw on these experiences, to appreciate the ways in which they differ from one another and to view these differences positively. We can develop an effective anti-discriminatory approach whatever the composition of the nursery/school i.e. whether the children are all White, all boys, all girls, all middle class, all abled, all from heterosexual families. The fact that they have opportunities to think about and to link their own experience to other inequalities is likely to be more effective than simply telling them about 'other' cultures.

Embedding anti-racism and multicultural education into nursery/ school ethos and practice gives all children the opportunity to develop to their maximum potential. By ensuring equal access and participation for all children, we contribute to the creation of a more just and equal society. An anti-discriminatory approach shapes policy and practice in a wide range of ways:

- Review and revise the organisation, management and ethos of the nursery/school and how we relate to the children, present material to them and encourage them to learn. Educational practices will be based on co-operation and power sharing.

• Acknowledge that the ethos of nurseries/schools may be discriminating against certain children and their families. Formulate and implement clear and effective equality policies in consultation with parents and relevant members of the community.

• Understand and accept that certain principles, like providing equal access, concern and treatment, are non-negotiable but that procedures and ways of achieving them are open to negotiation.

• Understand and accept that the imparting of 'cultural' knowledge does not in itself prepare children for life in a multi-ethnic society. When festivals like Chinese New Year and Hanukah are celebrated, it will be within an antiracist framework.

• Ensure that institutional practices like the recruitment, selection and promotion of staff and admission procedures for new children are fair and consistent.

• Examine and learn to understand the way various oppressions affect children and their families. For example, the lives of disabled children may be affected by not only their impairment but also by their ethnicity, class, and gender.

• Implement culturally appropriate curricula that include the past and present experiences and contributions to human progress of women and Black, working class, or disabled people. Equality issues will be part of the curriculum and raised whenever 'teachable moments' present themselves.

• Acknowledge the fact that very young children may pick up negative attitudes towards the adults and children against whom our society already discriminates. Intervene in the process by which young children begin learning that it is 'better' to be rich than to be poor, that it is 'better' to be White than Black and that it is 'better' to be a boy than a girl, so that the children are less likely to feel superior to others or internalise oppression.

Anti-discriminatory practice and a culturally appropriate curriculum equips educators and children to actively challenge inequality and injustice. This sound practice provides us with opportunities to value, praise, support and give intellectual stimulation and individual attention to every child in an environment in which the culture of each is appropriately reflected. Children will be enabled to retain their cultural integrity while gaining the skills and knowledge they need in the wider society. They will be helped to feel secure, to feel 'at home', to experience success whether they are high flyers or find learning difficult. Helen Penn (1997:8) quotes Loris Malaguzzi's view of children and the way they learn. He profoundly influenced the innovative early childhood practices in Reggio Emilia in North Italy:

> Our image of children no longer considers them as isolated and egocentric, does not only see them engaged in action with objects, does not emphasise only cognitive aspects, does not belittle feelings or what is not logical, and does not consider with ambiguity the role of the affective domain. Instead our image of the child is rich in potential, strong, powerful, competent and most of all, connected to adults and other children.

# Chapter 3

# Learning the anti-discriminatory way

*If we begin with our children and our grandchildren then we just might live to see a community and nation and world which respects and celebrates diversity, a world in which we all live together without prejudice, discrimination, bigotry and hate.* Source unknown

This chapter explores how we can reflect on our own educational practice, attitudes and feelings and build on our understanding, skills and knowledge so that children can learn from our example. Statements like 'I treat all children the same' and 'I don't know what colour my children are, I never notice,' are critically examined. Issues around resourcing for equality are discussed and a checklist is provided to indicate how successfully we are creating an anti-discriminatory environment.

Celebrating diversity within an anti-discriminatory framework is a rewarding and stimulating process that calls for flexibility, a willingness to consider and adopt new ideas, and sensitive understanding of children who are harassed because they are different. We need to be able to encourage children to see others as special, to enjoy learning about one another's lives and to appreciate the similarities and differences that exist between them. We need to help them understand why they should not hurt and tease each other about their differences but, rather, value and appreciate them.

Although racism is alive and well in Britain today the justifications for it have undergone subtle change. The 'problem' is nowadays expressed more in terms of cultural difference i.e. Black people have a different culture, a different life-style which is seen to be threatening British traditions and cultural heritage. The British way of life is considered to be in danger and in need of protection from 'alien' cultures. This anxiety was played upon by Margaret Thatcher in 1978 when she declared: *'People are really rather afraid that this country might be swamped by people with a different culture'*. Islam tends to be seen as the greatest threat (Runnymede Trust, 1997). That these views are widely held does not necessarily mean that all, or even most White educators agree with them but it is highly likely that everyone is influenced by them.

The trend toward formal teaching and the emphasis on narrowly defined academic skills makes it even more important to implement a culturally relevant curriculum that engages children's feelings, and that reflects and respects the lives, beliefs and experiences of girls and boys from various ethnic, social and cultural backgrounds and from a wide range of ability levels. It involves making decisions about what to teach, how to teach, when to teach it and how to evaluate the impact on children's learning. It is essential that we are aware of the 'hidden' curriculum. For instance:

What criteria do we use when we select books, toys and other learning resources?

How do our attitudes, assumptions and expectations of children and their parents affect the way we relate to them?

How do we group children and by what criteria do we choose them to do various activities or tasks?

How do we maintain discipline and what reward system do we use?

Much of children's learning is promoted through planned play activities. Play, according to Vygotsky, is a revolutionary activity because it involves original, creative ways of thinking in imaginative situations which in turn heighten cognitive performance. Through individual and group play children can learn and consolidate social and physical skills, share ideas, experiences and feelings, explore, experiment and create. We enrich the quality of their play and learning by providing a well-planned curriculum that effectively teaches children the skills and strategies they need, promotes problem solving and decision making, and strikes a balance between child-initiated and adult directed activities. It is accessible to everyone and enables all children to feel self-confident, proud of themselves and their families without feeling superior or inferior to others. A project on ourselves and other people, for example, could encourage all children to talk and to draw (older ones could write) about themselves – their names, their physical features, their family, their friends, their cultural practices, their favourite foods, music, toys and games.

When we work from an anti-discriminatory perspective we recognise the right of both girls and boys to have a curriculum that values each sex equally and gives equal opportunity to participate in all its aspects. Books, games and packaging are carefully selected in favour of those which portray both girls and boys as active and powerful. To broaden children's experience, women and men who are doing non-traditional jobs can be invited to come in to the nursery/school to talk to the children about their work. Children can be given opportunities to learn about women's and men's contribution to challenging discrimination and injustice. By celebrating special events like Women's Day on March 8th, children, educators and parents honour the women they know as well as famous women. Mother's Day can be celebrated by focusing on the work mothers do in and outside the home.

The individuality of children with developmental or physical impairment is respected and valued when the curriculum is based on a flexible approach to education and care. Appropriate expectations are set for each child and their educators have a sensitive awareness of their rights and needs. Inclusion of children with special needs hinges on our meeting the needs of all the children and adapting the curriculum accordingly.

## Developing understanding

We need to develop our own respect and appreciation for those who are different from ourselves and to be willing to discuss these differences openly. We require accurate information, sensitive awareness and commitment to counter discriminatory attitudes and practices. This may mean that there is much that we need to learn and much to be unlearned. For example, if we have grown up thinking that men, White people and abled people are superior to everyone else then we may well give children a distorted view of life and a false picture of the world. So we need time to reflect continually on our own attitudes, feelings and practice and seize opportunities to learn about and appreciate a variety of life-styles and the contribution that Black people, women, people with disabilities and working class men and women have made and are making to human progress. As suggested in chapter seven, ongoing inservice anti-discriminatory training can provide knowledge and expertise and help develop the confidence all this demands. However, although excellent training opportunities are available, lack of funding and staff cuts prevent many hard-working, stressed-out educators from taking advantage of them.

For those who may not have much experience of working from an anti-discriminatory perspective, a good place to begin is to learn about and take pride in their own cultures and then inform themselves about the cultures of the children in the nursery/school. It may come as a surprise to find how much our own prejudices and training get in the way of being prepared to accept new ideas, try new ways of doing things, taste different foods, listen to unfamiliar music, and learn other languages. Developing sensitive awareness and commitment to counter racism and other forms of discrimination is vital. Lack of appropriate knowledge and a fixed belief in the superiority of their own cultural practices may cause White educators to act in a racist way, consciously or unconsciously, as the following examples illustrate:

> An Asian child was busy pretending to make tea in the home corner.
>
> A member of staff intervened. 'No dear, we don't use the saucepan, we use the teapot.'
>
> The little girl was going to make tea in the way her mother did at home – boiling the tea, milk and sugar together in a saucepan. She was left feeling frustrated, bewildered and wondering why her mother didn't know how to make tea properly.

...ent described by Iram Siraj-Blatchford (1991:12) highlights the importance of involving non-teaching staff in discussions and in-service training:

> In an infant school a four-year old continued to struggle with a knife and fork at lunch times over a period of several weeks. At home his parents ate Pakistani food, chapattis and rice were eaten by hand, as is normal practice. The child was learning for the first time that food could be eaten using implements other than hands. The teachers encouraged his development. One lunch time, after struggling to balance baked beans on his fork for some time, he resorted to using his hands. The school secretary (who collected payment for meals in the hall) shouted across the hall to this little boy, 'Stop eating with your hands, only animals eat with their hands!' The look on the four-year-old's face was one of bewilderment, hurt and embarrassment. She had indicated that not only was his behaviour deviant and animal-like, but by implication so was his parents' and that of the community.

Headteachers too may be unaware and ill-informed – as this incident that I witnessed illustrates:

> The Head of a junior school in the North of England was conducting an assembly on Diwali. The previous week he had admitted Asian twins from a practising Muslim family. He now turned to them and asked them to tell all the children what they did at home to celebrate Diwali. The bewildered children remained silent and the Headteacher, interpreted their silence as shyness. It was later pointed out to him by their class teacher that Diwali is a Hindu festival so would not be celebrated by Muslims.

## The dangers of a 'White is best' approach

There is an argument that educators can create a neutral environment in which children's natural innocence is being preserved and in which all have the same opportunity to blossom. But is it possible to create a neutral environment? Don't personal values and beliefs inevitably creep in and actively influence the content and the way equipment and learning activities are presented to children? Isn't it likely that the 'neutral' environment reflects the educator's view of the world and the people in it?

χ  The claim to 'treat children all the same' is neither likely nor desirable. Children's stage of development, their abilities, individual likes and dislikes, strengths and weaknesses all influence the way they are treated. It is generally accepted that aggressive children need to be responded to differently from those who are withdrawn and that new children need to be treated differently from 'old-timers'. Treating all children in the same way and ignoring their differences might, unwittingly, be putting pressure on children to deny their differences so that they can be the 'same' as those in the dominant group. Rejecting part of themselves in this way can seriously affect children's sense of identity and self-worth. Similarly, working with Black and White children and sincerely believing that the colour of their skin is irrelevant because they are all just children and so should all be treated alike runs the risk of equating, 'they are all the same' with 'they are all White'. The Swann Report (1985:26) calls this the 'colour-blind' approach:

> ... many of the teachers to whom we spoke on our visits were at pains to assert that they deliberately made no distinction between 'black' pupils and others: they were 'colour blind'. In this way they claimed to fulfill the first duty of a teacher which they saw as regarding all pupils equally ... We ourselves regard 'colour-blindness' however as potentially just as negative as a straightforward rejection of people with a different skin colour since both types of attitude seek to deny the validity of an important aspect of a person's identity.

Implicit in the colour-blind approach is the assumption that White customs, traditions and way of life are the 'right ones' and that others, being different, are not quite as 'good' – a superior attitude that is perfectly conveyed in this extract from a rhyme popular in the 1930s,

> *And if they all were English, it would save a lot of fuss,*
> *And wouldn't it be nice for them, if they were all like us?*

Adopting a 'colour-blind' approach is likely to reinforce White children's feelings of superiority, deny the life experiences of Black children, miseducate everyone and arouse responses like this one quoted by Ramdeen (1988:29):

My teacher is always telling me that she does not see my colour and that she treats all the children the same. If she does not see my colour then she does not see *ME*.

In their study Ogilvy and others (1990) showed that although educators in multi-ethnic Scottish nurseries thought that they treated the children according to their individual needs, observations and videotapes of interactions between adults and children showed that South Asian children were given less attention, were spoken to less and that staff used poor models of English when explaining things to them. This practice was also noted by Biggs and Edwards (1992:163):

> Teachers were found to interact less frequently with black children than with white, they had fewer exchanges lasting more than thirty seconds with black children, they also spent less time with them discussing the particular task which had been set.

Treating children 'all the same' ignores the very differences that make them unique individuals. It is the opposite of an anti-discriminatory approach in which they are treated equally, with equal concern and their different needs – psychological, cultural and social – are recognised and responded to. This approach encourages children to learn about and value each other's cultures, languages, abilities and life-styles and draw strength from their own. The criteria suggested by the Schools Council and endorsed and extended in the Swann Report (1985:329) provide a useful guide:

I. The variety of social, cultural and ethnic groups and a perspective of the world should be evident in visuals, stories, conversation and information.

II. People from social, cultural and ethnic groups should be presented as individuals with every human attribute.

III. Cultures should be empathetically described in their own terms and not judged against some notion of 'ethnocentric' or 'euro-centric' culture.

IV. The curriculum should include accurate information on racial and cultural differences and similarities.

We strongly support these criteria but would wish to add a further two ...

- All children should be encouraged to see cultural diversity in a positive light.

- The issue of racism, at both institutional and individual level, should be considered openly and efforts made to counter it.

## Inequality and diversity: Black children

To support children's learning we need to be alert to the obvious and subtle discriminatory factors in society and the nursery/school. Many developmental tests, for example, are culturally biased because they are standardised on White, middle class children and may include toys and equipment unfamiliar to Black and working class children. Assessments based on such tests may therefore be inaccurate. For example, a three year old girl was given a doll's table, chairs and a small tablecloth, which she used to wipe her nose instead of putting it on the table. She knew about handkerchiefs but not about tablecloths! Measuring certain accomplishments to assess children's developmental progress might well be inappropriate. The ability to handle a knife and fork is likely to be less developed in children whose families traditionally eat with their hands or chopsticks, so they could be incorrectly assessed. Jennie Lindon (1993) points out that eating with a knife and fork is still listed in some development charts or guidelines. It's also possible that we might not appreciate that children learning English as an additional language may understand the concepts involved in assessment tests but not have the English vocabulary they need. A more accurate result could be obtained if the tests were administered to the children in their home language. The next chapter is devoted to language issues.

Most of us help children to value their own and a range of cultural traditions. However, we may not have realised the conflict that children exposed to racism experience. Morgan (1996:39) suggests that:

> Children of African-Caribbean heritage in Britain are caught up between two cultures, one which they see devalued and the other with which they do not fully identify but which is seen as superior by society. Just coping with being Black and watching and listening as society devalues us can be stressful and contribute to low self-esteem, poor motivation, depression and even anti-social behaviour.

## THE SHADOW

A lonely figure enters.
>He produces a ball.
>'Anyone want to play?'
>They turn away,
>He is different.

'My father told me to stay clear of them sort'.
He moves towards the playground wall
He knows each red brick almost by name
The wall is his friend.
He scratches his curly black hair
>'Go back to where you came from!'
>The daily chant begins
>He closes his ears
>and moves on.

School finishes
At the back of the bus queue he stands
>desolate and alone
>His expressionless face
>disguises the day's deep damage
>like a veil.

He climbs the stairs to his humble flat,
>the lift is out of order
>He reaches for his key, enters
He greets his mother and his sister
>goes quickly to his room.
>He covers his black face
>with his black hands
>and cries softly into the pillow
>which knows his tears so well.

This poem, written by a 14 year old underlines how important it is to intervene when children are called names, teased or are physically abused.

Never underestimate how overwhelming feelings of isolation, alienation, anger, bewilderment and rejection can be for children who are
harassed or excluded from play, nor the extent to which their learning
can be affected when they are unhappy, angry, or anxious. This tale was
told to me by a friend of the family.

> A five year old Sikh boy had eagerly anticipated starting infant school
> but within months of his being a pupil at the school, he radically
> changed from being active, bright and outgoing, into a withdrawn child
> no longer communicating with anyone, wetting himself and having
> nightmares. A few sessions at a clinic revealed that he was frightened
> to go to school because the other children teased him for wearing a
> 'handkerchief' and mocked his grandfather who wore a turban when
> he brought him to school each morning. The school did not seem to con-
> sider that it was its responsibility to challenge the racist behaviour of the
> pupils and so did nothing. The head teacher advised the parents, 'to
> transfer him to another school where there were more Asian children.'

## Inequality and diversity: refugees

We need to know how to help the refugee children in nursery/school,
especially those who have fled a war zone, repression or organised
violence. Jill Rutter (1994), the Education Officer for the Refugee
Council advises that we should find out about the political situation in
the country from which families have fled and try and understand the
experiences they have gone through and the difficulties involved in
settling in a strange, often hostile, environment. We may need to try
various strategies to give these children the emotional support they
need, help them deal with their feelings and gain their trust and
confidence.

## Inequality and diversity: girls and boys

Educators may be surprised to learn that we need to help young children understand that being a girl or a boy depends on their anatomy and
not on the games they play, the clothes they wear or their hairstyles.
Children who are happy to play in non-stereotypical ways need
encouragement and support and all should be helped to counter stereotypes.

Sometimes, though, they sort things out for themselves, as this child from a nursery school in Scotland did:

> Four year old James was washing a doll.
>
> Robert said to him, 'Ooooh – only girls play with dolls.'
>
> 'It's fun with all the bubbles,' James replied.
>
> Robert looked at him, at the teacher who was standing nearby and went over to the water, watched James for a bit, then tentatively picked up a doll and joined in.

Girls do not always have the freedom, space, time and support to experience and learn a range of skills and become confident. We might need to devise ways to encourage them to join in physical activities like climbing, kicking balls and riding bikes. This may be complicated by the fact that boys tend to take up space as of right and to monopolise the equipment.

We might be unconsciously sending sexist messages by, for example, allowing rowdiness and fighting from boys, but intervening if girls fight or are rowdy. We may not cuddle boys as often as girls or encourage them to express their feelings and be gentle with one another. We may not reassure them that it is alright for boys to cry but it is important to do so because they seldom see men behaving in this way.

The words we use can influence children's play choices. For example, if we call the home corner the 'dramatic play area' and resource it suitably then some of the boys who feel they have no role in the 'home corner' may play in it. By encouraging boys and girls to play in a wide variety of imaginative scenarios such as hospitals, factories, space ships, trailers, garages; and to use the dressing-up clothes, jewellery, hats, wigs; and by providing tool chests, hard hats, overalls and other work-related clothes, we can help children change stereotyped attitudes they may already hold.

Debbie Epstein (1995:63) suggests that these strategies are insufficient in themselves. She argues that children are strongly wedded to their gender beliefs i.e. what it means to be a boy or a girl, as these help them to make sense of themselves She maintains that providing boys and girls with positive images and role models and helping them to recognise and challenge discrimination needs to be set in a context in which they are offered alternative understandings of what it means to be a boy and what it means to be a girl. Her interpretation of the following incident helps to crystallise her approach:

> Clare, Becky and Natasha came to see me with a complaint: they were being prevented from playing with the large bricks by Michael, Nathan and Ben. Furthermore, said Clare, Michael says girls don't play bricks. If I want to play in the bricks I must be a boy! Clare was extremely upset, more by the accusation of being a boy than being denied the chance to play with the bricks (though she wanted to do that as well). She clearly felt that being told she must be a boy was one of the worst insults that could be thrown at her and perhaps this is not surprising in the light of young children's attachment to gender difference (and in the light of the intended insult).

Epstein's response was to introduce times in the week when only the girls could play with the bricks. Their constructions related to domestic play and fairy tales, which she noted, enabled them to hold on to their 'girlish' ways and at the same time challenge stereotypes of what it means to be a girl. The girls were very proud of the large and complicated palace they built. It was much admired and Michael, who had initially not wanted the girls to play with the bricks, dictated the following diary entry: *I used to think girls don't do bricks. They made really good houses, specially Clare. Now I like to play with Clare in the bricks. We make lots of good buildings.* Epstein never saw them building together but she argues that the fact that he now wanted to include Clare in a 'masculine' activity was an important breakthrough.

A teacher I know, working in an infant school in Liverpool, sought to provide experiences that might offer children alternative understandings. She gave her class of top infants an activity which, she hoped, would encourage them to see themselves and each other through different eyes and to learn from one another.

> The children were asked to draw their very own dream ship in which they could travel wherever they wanted to. The teacher explained that they should draw it so that everyone could see what was inside it – like a doll's house with the front opened. Not surprisingly, the boys had guns and radar as well as engines or sails on their ships. One boy

included a fridge with beer in it. The girls concentrated on the living quarters, papering the walls, providing kitchens with appliances and food, and one girl even put in a sick bay. The pictures were then put on the walls for the children to look at. During the ensuing discussion the boys poured scorn on the girls because none of them had provided their ships with engines and one had given hers wheels. They stopped laughing when it was pointed out that they would have had a very uncomfortable voyage as they had nowhere to sit or sleep and they would have died of hunger and thirst.

To try and break down girls' stereotypical play, Ross and Browne (1993) propose a very different strategy. They recommend removing the windows, doors, floor and 'play people' from construction sets like lego so as to encourage girls to use the materials in different ways rather than constructing houses and playing 'families'.

## Inequality and diversity: Traveller children
Whether or not there are Traveller children in the group, we need to appreciate that they are discriminated against largely because of their nomadic life-style. Laws banishing 'Gypsies' (most prefer the term Travellers) and threatening anyone associating with them with death were passed under Henry VIII in the 16th century and only repealed in the late 18th century. Attitudes are deep-rooted. Consequently, opportunities should be provided to talk about any negative feelings we may have. Learning about how Traveller families live may dispel myths that we might have unconsciously absorbed. Many Travellers live in houses but, as Brian Foster (1993:54) describes, others live in trailers:

> Traveller camps are not random groups of individual families in individual trailers. ... children grow up in a large, close-knit community, surrounded by grandparents, aunts, uncles, cousins and siblings. This community offers care, support and education, and can help share and dissipate the tensions which prejudice and hostility can generate.

James Coyle (1996:14) writes: *I live with my mum and dad and three brothers. It is cosy and warm in our trailer. We have a chimney, a fridge and a television. We have two bedrooms.*

Michael McDonagh (1996:51) writes:

> I like this school. I have lived in thirteen houses and a lot of sites, one in Dublin. I had two big dogs, Lassie and Wolf. My sisters go to school and my big sister goes to secondary school and her reading is good. I live in a house in Tottenham and I have been in this school for a year now. I have lots of friends, Jamil, Kelvin, Mattie, Michael and Daniel. They know I am a Traveller and they like me. I play football with them. I have a good teacher and a teacher for Travellers comes in to see me every week. A lady called Ivy helps me as well. I am better at reading and I have good writing. I can sound out letters and make words. I like the computer. In my last school the children were not nice to me and I was fighting a lot. Here I have learned to get on better with other children. I like school.

If children from Traveller families are about to join the nursery/school it is important that we find out whether they live in houses or trailers. For those who live in trailers starting nursery/school can be a traumatic experience because it could be the first time that they have been in a large indoor space or encountered running water and flushing toilets. The concept of looking after play materials may be new to them because at home they may play with scrap metals and other odds and ends which are then discarded. As their parents may be illiterate and their access to books and writing materials limited, the children's reading and writing readiness may be less developed than most children from settled communities. Providing suitable play materials and books which depict trailers and other features of the Traveller way of life can help Traveller children feel more comfortable and enable everyone to enjoy and benefit from the experiences being offered. As with all families, each Traveller family will have its own history and experiences, beliefs and values which need to be understood to ensure that the provision is culturally appropriate. Parents and the children themselves are the best source of such information. Setting up a trailer home corner and themes such as transport, working animals or homes can easily be integrated into a culturally appropriate curriculum.

## Inequality and diversity: disabled children

It may be difficult for abled educators to appreciate the extent to which
the lives of most disabled children are defined by their disability or the
degree to which their needs, desires and hopes get pushed to one side.
Black children's disability can also take centre stage, thus marginalis-
ing racism, which means that a significant part of their identity and
their needs may be ignored and unmet. The presence of disabled children in the nursery/school may be the first time that educators come
into close contact with a child who has a physical or learning disability.
The generally accepted principle, 'build on what children can do' is
particularly relevant and important because disabled children need to
have their abilities focused on, not their disabilities. They need time to
develop at their own pace and to have access to equipment and
materials with different textures and tactile qualities as well as those
that require varying degrees of manual dexterity. While we juggle with
tight budgets we may need to remind ourselves that such resources
benefit both the disabled and the abled children. To encourage physically disabled and abled children to interact with and learn from one
another, we may have to rearrange the room so that all areas and equipment, toys and activities are easily accessible. For example, cushions
and large bean-bags may be needed to provide extra support if activities are on the floor. A valuable lesson that we and the children can
learn is that nobody is perfect, everyone is impaired in some way.

## Inequality and diversity: children from homosexual families

We may feel uncomfortable about addressing issues around sexuality
because in many cultures and religions homosexuality is not accepted
or is considered to be a sin. We may share the concerns of many parents
that having a book about a lesbian or gay family will promote homosexuality or that boys wearing skirts and playing with dolls will encourage them to 'grow up queer'. Opportunities may need to be provided to enable staff and parents to express such anxieties, to be reassured that children benefit from this type of play and to understand
that encouraging gender equality can extend the emotional, social and
cognitive development of all children. Some educators may be shocked
to discover that they are working with lesbian and gay colleagues or

with children from lesbian and gay families who, because of attitudes towards homosexuality, may be living with a 'secret'. Their parents need to know that hurtful comments and name-calling would be routinely challenged and that we will constantly check that the language and the resources we use do not only reflect the 'ideal' family of biological mother, father and 2.2 children. Patrick and Burke (1993:201) quote Ackroy, a lesbian mother and educationalist:

> I want primary teachers to inform children about alternatives to the nuclear family and to integrate this into all their work concerning home backgrounds. I want them to use the words 'lesbian' and 'gay' and to present them as a valid personal and political identity (and not a sexual act).

## Resourcing for change

For parents or children who come into nurseries/schools in which their cultures are not being acknowledged and represented, it is like looking in a mirror and not seeing a reflection. To ensure that conscious and unconscious racism, sexism, class, ablism and homophobia are eliminated and that all children's general knowledge, imagination and self-esteem are fostered, resources need to be continually reviewed and evaluated. Concern stems from the fact that children can pick up negative messages about themselves and others through the resources they encounter. Some manufacturers and publishers are producing toys, books and other learning materials which challenge stereotypes and present positive images of and for all children. But there are not enough of them and their products tend to be on sale in specialist shops or only a few High Street shops. We educators can order these resources through catalogues but they are not generally available to parents. Chapter eight offers information about some of the suppliers whose products counter discrimination and promote respect for a range of life-styles and cultures.

To extend the range of resources being presented to children and to show them that the nursery/school values diversity, we can invite parents to contribute their knowledge and skills to help produce appropriate books and wall displays. The teaching of numeracy could include different ways of counting – on the fingers, on the knuckles –

and equipment that various cultures use, such as the abacus, could be provided. Children are likely to enjoy the experience of carefully examining textiles produced and decorated in various ways from many parts of the world, such as Peruvian weaving and knitting, mirror-work from India and the Middle East, cotton batiks from Africa. These can then be appropriately incorporated into the general resources in the nursery/school.

Remember that even when all toys and other learning materials have been carefully chosen, the critical issue is *how* they are used. Resources and the way they are presented can enable children to see beyond society's definition of who and what is generally accepted as beautiful. They can help them to value and respect various shades of skin colour, a variety of hair textures and facial features, and a range of body shapes. When we adopt this approach and provide positive images we reduce the scope for ridicule and feelings of superiority and help to promote self-respect and pride.

If our society were free of discrimination we would not need to be so concerned about the fact that, for example, there are so many positive images of White people and of abled people but so few of Black people and of disabled people. Resources that feature Black people are generally thought to be *for* Black children and the importance of providing them for White children is seldom recognised. Similarly, the few that feature disabled children are seldom found in nurseries/schools where there are only abled children.

One image that definitely does not belong in any nursery/school is the golliwog. It reinforces a negative stereotype of Black people as being comical, foolish and unattractive. In the Oxford dictionary it is defined as: 'a grotesque doll with fuzzy hair, round eyes, thickened lips and fixed grin'. Do you know that the abusive term 'wog' is derived from the golliwog? There is a further twist. At the beginning of this century when Jewish people were fleeing to Britain to escape a series of pogroms in Eastern Europe, a new toy made its appearance – a hooked nose and leering features were stamped on to the head and body of the golliwog.

In Enid Blyton's original stories about three golliwogs, the negative qualities attributed to darkness, i.e. fear and danger, are also applied to them and none of the other toys play with them because their mistress, Angela, does not like their black faces. To add insult to injury, nine of the eleven stories are based on mistaken identity – the three golliwogs all look alike.

Golliwogs don't only appear in stories. The image is still featured on fabrics like curtaining material and on Robertson's jam jars. Although the 'golly' is remembered with affection by some White and a few Black adults, many Black parents vividly recall their pain and humiliation when, as children, they were taunted about golliwogs and compared to them. They don't want their children to be submitted to similar ordeals.

We should be sure to give children the message that even though members of a particular culture share certain common beliefs and practices, there are considerable variations. Not all Hindu women wear saris, not all Greek families attend the Orthodox Church, not all Jewish men and boys wear skullcaps and not all African people are good at or even interested in music. Focusing on differences while ignoring similarities and overlooking the differences between people from the same group does little to eradicate stereotypes.

Care needs to be taken that the dressing-up clothes represent the everyday clothes from a range of cultures rather than 'national costumes'. Consultation with parents can ensure that resources do in fact reflect the life-styles of the children. A useful strategy was adopted by educators in an Australian nursery school I visited:

> They knew from experience that although there were great similarities within an ethnic group, each family practised its culture in its own way and that there could be differences in their child-rearing practices. When a number of Vietnamese children were admitted, they asked each of the Vietnamese parents about what to them was meaningful and relevant in their culture. Armed with this information they were then able to introduce a Vietnamese perspective into their provision which was culturally appropriate for all the children.

For many children the experience of being cared for and educated outside their home is a culture shock. Only when we appreciate this will we be ready and able to support them. How might children feel coming into an environment in which the adults and all or most of the children have a different skin colour, the women wear quite different clothes from those worn by women in their family and communities, and the equipment, especially in the home corner, is unfamiliar? By empathising with and supporting children who are disabled and adapting our provision and practice accordingly we can help them feel more comfortable. We may need to give children who live in cramped conditions opportunities and space to enable them to play freely, to make a noise and to express their feelings. For many parents handing their children over to us arouses anxiety and concern – we are after all strangers. The likelihood that they and their children will have a positive experience in the nursery/school depends to a large extent on how welcome we make them feel. We need to create an environment where children can develop skills, confidence in their own talents and respect for others, and in which policy and practice recognise and counteract stereotyping and celebrate diversity. To do this successfully we need to look at our own practice.

## An opportunity to rate yourself

You can gain a sense of whether you are creating an anti-discriminatory environment by rating yourself on this checklist. For each statement ring the words that best describe your provision and practice.

In my workplace I use resources and provide activities that reflect and teach about:

1.  all the children and their families in my group

    often          sometimes          never

2.  children and adults from the main ethnic groups living in the vicinity of the nursery/school

    often          sometimes          never

3.  a range of languages especially those spoken by parents and children in the nursery/school

    often          sometimes          never

4.  people from class, cultural and ethnic backgrounds that are different from my own without encouraging or reinforcing stereotypical thinking

    often          sometimes          never

5.  a range of families including single mothers or fathers, mothers in jobs outside the home and fathers at home, fathers in jobs outside the home and mothers at home, families with two mothers or two fathers, middle class and working class families, families with differently able members and those with members from different ethnic and cultural groups

    often          sometimes          never

6.  Black and White women and men doing a range of tasks in the home

    often          sometimes          never

7.  differently abled people at work, at leisure and being with their families

    often          sometimes          never

8.  people from different backgrounds who contribute, or have contributed to our lives, including those who have been involved in the fight for justice.

    often          sometimes          never

Now total your points and examine the results:
For every **often** answer give yourself 2 points.
For every **sometimes** answer give yourself 1 point.
For every **never** answer give yourself 0 points.

If you scored between **14 and 16** you are using an anti-discriminatory approach

If you scored between **11 and 13** you are using an anti-discriminatory approach in some areas

If you scored between **5 and 10** you are introducing cultural activities and celebrations at special times, seeing other cultures as 'exotic' and not incorporating them into all aspects of the programme. This approach doesn't give children the tools they need to interact comfortably, empathically and fairly with diversity.

If your score is **4 or below**, you are reflecting and teaching from the dominant culture's viewpoint and ignoring the experiences and views of people from groups different from your own.

# Chapter 4

# Language Matters

*Children of minority and indigenous populations shall freely enjoy their own culture, religion and language.* United Nations Declaration on the Rights of the Child

This chapter highlights the power of language. As languages spoken by Black people tend to be viewed negatively there are implications for the teaching of English as an additional language to Black children. Providing a multilingual environment for all children familiarises them with a range of languages, extends their general knowledge, motivates them to learn languages different from their own and positively influences their attitudes to people different from themselves.

It is largely through language that adults and children formulate and express their thoughts and make sense of their world. Moreover, how people speak 'classifies' them i.e. it reveals their class and ethnic background and where they come from as surely as the clothes they wear or the neighbourhood they live in. Judgements that are based on the way colleagues, children and parents speak influence, often unconsciously, how we relate to and communicate with them.

From a linguistic point of view all community languages are equal. Linguists have not been able to find a language that is primitive, inadequate or deficient. It is factually incorrect to describe some languages, for example, Spanish or Swedish as 'better' or 'more developed' than

Chinese or Creole. Nevertheless languages spoken by White people continue to be considered superior to languages spoken by Black people, for example, European languages like French, German and Italian are accorded a higher status than Arabic, Hindi or Swahili. Experiments described by Edwards (1995:7) bear this out. In one:

> Student teachers judged recordings of a middle class White boy, a working class White girl, a recently arrived Jamaican girl and a British born girl from a Barbadian background who spoke twice – once using a working class English accent and once a Barbadian dialect. The middle class boy was consistently evaluated most favourably: he was felt to be more intelligent, better behaved and so on. Next came the two working class recordings, one White, the other Black, followed by the two Caribbean children. The crucial point is that the same child was judged more positively in her English than in her Caribbean 'guise'. The student teachers were also prepared to make judgements about the children's educational outcomes, predicting high academic success for the middle class boy and very low levels of achievement for the Black children.

> In the second experiment many different language varieties were used including French, English, Greek, Yiddish and African American English. In all cases, the judges listened to recorded speech, unaware that one of the speakers was heard twice over, once using the high status variety, the second time the low status variety. In every case, speakers of the high status dialect or language were considered to be more intelligent and competent.

Smith (1997) reported a preliminary study conducted at Worcester College of Higher Education where male actors were hired to reproduce police interviews with suspected armed robbers and cheque fraudsters. The actors used the Birmingham or 'Brummie' accent and standard accents and the suspect's guilt was judged by 119 students. One of the researchers, Berenice Mahoney, (1997:9) said, '*The Brummie suspect was regarded as less intelligent, more likely to be poor and working class and less socially competent*'.

# The power of language

In English the word 'black' has many negative associations eg. black-leg, black mood, whereas the word 'white' tends to be associated with purity and goodness. Language describes, categorises and labels people. It can be used to value them and challenge stereotypes but it can also reinforce stereotypes, belittle individuals and groups and help to maintain oppressive attitudes and practices. For example, there are many words and terms that women find insulting like: bitch, silly cow, fat slob. Language also encourages sexist stereotyping when, for instance, jobs and roles are described in terms of men such as 'man-power', 'the man-in-the-street', 'man-to-man'. Alternatives like 'workforce', 'an ordinary person', 'face-to-face', can change perceptions. Using the pronoun he to refer to doctors and pilots and she to nurses and cleaners, perpetuates and strengthens stereotypes.

Black adults and children including those of mixed parentage are hurt and demeaned when people use words like Paki, Coloured, Half-caste. However, covert language, less easy to identify, is also used, for example referring to Black people as immigrants, foreigners, aliens, and asking them where they are from. This assumes that Black people are not British – even though most are British born. It is quite possible that their Britishness is acknowledged only when they travel in other countries!

Certain words and phrases, like, 'culturally deprived', 'language deficient', 'violent' and 'aggressive' are so often associated with Black and working class children, especially boys, that they become code words i.e. even though neither 'Black' nor 'working class' is mentioned, most people know that these are the children being described. Similarly, suggests David Gillborn (1994), talk of 'the nation', 'our heritage' and 'tradition' often operate as a code for 'race' issues and potentially racist policies can be presented in non-racist terms so they appear neutral and fair. He argues that the National Curriculum emphasises 'the nation's Christian heritage and traditions' and although it was introduced as an aid to 'every child in the community' in *reality* it excludes many children and their communities.

No terms are 'right' forevermore. Adults' and children's perceptions of themselves are influenced by the way society perceives them so the terms they use to refer to themselves or the group(s) to which they

**Tomorrow I am going to re-write the English language** by Lois Keith
Tomorrow I am going to re-write the English language
I will discard all those striving ambulist metaphors
Of power and success
And construct new images to describe my strength
My new, different strength.

Then I won't have to feel dependent
Because I can't Stand On My Own Two Feet
And I will refuse to feel a failure
Because I didn't Stay One Step Ahead.
I won't feel inadequate
When I don't Stand Up For Myself
or illogical because I cannot
Just Take it One Step at a Time

I will make them understand that it is a very male way
To describe the world
All this Walking Tall
And Making Great Strides.

Yes, tomorrow I am going to re-write the English Language,
Creating the world in my own image.
Mine will be a gentler, more womanly way
To describe my progress.
I will wheel, cover and encircle
Somehow I will learn to say it all.

belong and which they prefer other people to use change as conditions and perceptions change.

Within a single group one person may favour a term which another considers offensive so it is possible to use terms without realising that they can cause offence. We need constantly to check with the people concerned that the terms we use are appropriate. For example, most disabled people are offended by terms like 'handicap', 'handicapped person', 'cripple', and 'retarded'. They prefer: disability, disabled person, mobility impaired, or learning difficulty. They object to being described as being 'spastic', 'deaf and dumb', 'Mongoloid', or as 'the Blind' or 'the Deaf' and prefer being referred to as having Cerebral

Palsy, Downs' Syndrome, as a blind or partially sighted person, or as a deaf or partially hearing person.

To try and avoid using language that bolsters sexist attitudes, Browne and France (1985) developed a helpful strategy. They monitored their own and their colleagues language and then recorded and analysed the most common labels and phrases they used to describe girls and boys as well as the content of their conversations with them. They were shocked to find that girls were being described for instance as 'bossy' whereas boys were 'born leaders'.

Jennie Lindon (1993:17) reminds us that:

> Helping children learn is a challenge for adults. How adults behave and how they speak with children will be very important. Exactly the same words could be spoken by two different adults and yet the first person might, by the tone of voice and other body language, convey a very encouraging message and the second could sound grudging and ultimately discouraging.

## Breaking language barriers

Given appropriate opportunities, encouragement, and time to achieve competence, young children are capable of learning two or more languages without becoming confused or overloaded. Edwards (1995:6) comments that whether bilingualism is viewed as a problem depends on who the children are:

> Bilingualism has not proved to be a problem for children from English speaking homes attending either Welsh schools or French immersion programs in Canada. The critical difference between French-English and Welsh-English bilinguals, on the one hand, and Bengali-English or Panjabi-English bilinguals, on the other is that, in one case, the children learning a second language belong to a high status group and, in the other, they come from a low status group.

British children who are fluent in their home language(s) and in English do not require or receive the same support and guidance as children who are learning English as an additional language – emergent bilingual learners. Those from White minority ethnic groups for whom

English is an additional language are less likely than Black children to encounter negative and discriminatory attitudes because their home languages are more likely to be valued and respected. The focus in the rest of this chapter will, therefore, be on Black bilingual learners and not on the very large number of children from White minority ethnic groups who are learning English as an additional language.

Approximately 70% of the world's population is bilingual or multi-lingual i.e. able to communicate in more than one language, and linguistic and cultural diversity is the norm in most industrialised societies. Research constantly confirms the fact that failure to provide effectively for children who are learning the dominant language as an additional language produces low academic achievement and wastes human resources (Edwards, 1998). This key challenge is being met in different ways in different countries. Australia and the Netherlands, for example, provide state funding to support additional language learners whereas in Denmark home language teaching is excluded from the mainstream school curriculum. In other countries, like Catalonia a more structured immersion approach is adopted which aims to develop equal ease in Catalan, which most children learn as an additional language, and their home languages.

In Britain the official and primary reason for supporting and using children's home languages is to help them learn English as quickly as possible. Home languages are seen as positive assets for the fostering of 'the linguistic, religious and cultural identities of ethnic minority communities'. The key to equality of opportunity and academic success is enabling them to gain a good command of English. It is not seen as the role of the school to maintain minority ethnic languages. The emphasis is on the learning of English from and with their peers. Arriving at nursery/school, children are not assessed to determine their ability to use their home languages. According to Cummins (1984) this can have serious implications because children whose home language is well established are more likely to reach a similar level in their additional language. He argues that for many children the initial emphasis in the early years needs to be on the development of their home languages and not on the learning of English.

Experience in multilingual countries like Switzerland indicates that children will learn the dominant language more easily if their home language is well established and valued and research confirms this. The ground-breaking Mother Tongue Teaching Project MOTET in Bradford in 1987 highlighted the fact that when Panjabi and English speakers were given the opportunity to use their home language and were taught in it half the time and in English the other half, they performed better not only in English but also in other areas of the curriculum. This finding has implications for parents whose home language(s) are not English and who believe that their language(s) are not as suitable as English as a medium of instruction in nurseries/schools. Many feel that fluency in English is the only way that their children will be able to succeed, so want their children to learn English to the exclusion of their home language. They are usually relieved and happy to hear that the more effectively children are able to communicate in their home language, the easier it will be for them to learn an additional language. Other parents are worried that they will not be able to encourage their children to use their home language once they have learnt to speak English. Maureen Turner (1997:138) quotes an interview which suggests some positive steps that parents can take. Rameen is the only Urdu speaking child in her Infant school:

> We talked about the language spoken at home and the importance of continuing Rameen's first language. Rameen's mother was already sharing books with her in both Urdu and English. Rameen had had some dual-language books in the nursery and they both enjoyed using them. Rameen's mother was pleased to be reassured that Rameen was not going to be confused by speaking Urdu; she had felt that it was sad, but inevitable, that Urdu would be eroded by the dominant 'school' language. She was interested to hear that it would be useful to talk about number work and class topics in Urdu, to help Rameen to sort out her ideas in her stronger language.

Children growing up and speaking more than one language are also understanding different ways of thinking which, given appropriate encouragement, will help to boost their academic achievement. According to Vygotsky (1986) this is because language is our most powerful tool and our greatest asset. If we have a good grasp of language then we also have a sound ability to think because language and thought are so closely interwoven and can't be separated. Dulcie Engel and Marian Whitehead (1996:36) draw attention to the fact that:

> They [children learning English as an additional language] are aware that there is not necessarily a one-to-one correspondence between objects in the real world and the labels we attach to them: a four-legged animal that barks can be 'dog' or 'perro' depending on the audience or the setting ... they accept cultural differences more readily.

Having a good grasp of their own language and culture has a positive effect on intellectual development, helps develop early literacy and build confidence and self-esteem. With increased confidence in their own ethnicity, children soon realise that English is useful when they are in the outside world and that they need their home languages when they are praying, visiting relatives or taking part in communal activities. Problems and difficulties arise if we believe that maintaining children's home languages will limit the learning of English and if we have absorbed the racist belief that the English language is 'better' than others, especially those spoken by Black adults and children. The Swann Report (1985:386) claims that 'linguistic prejudice' directed at Black community languages contributes to their low status.

> When such attitudes exist in a school environment, not only on the part of teachers but also ethnic majority pupils, and are left uncorrected, and also permeate much of the policy making field, it is inevitable that the educational experience of an ethnic minority child for whom English is not a first language may be influenced in a very direct and immediate manner.

Many years have passed since the Swann Report came out but comments like the following recently made by an educator in a family centre illustrate that these attitudes persist and that as educators we may, consciously or unconsciously, be passing views like these to children:

> 'I'm really worried about Rehana. I've told her mother so often to speak to her in English but she doesn't listen. We can't communicate with Rehana, she can't play with the other children and she can't understand a single word at story time or at any other time for that matter.'

In her study of primary schools, Cecile Wright (1991:18) observed that some of the teachers were upset when Asian children spoke in their own languages and told them to stop. When encouraging them to participate, the teachers often communicated with them in basic telegraphic language. When they got no response they quickly lost patience and ignored them. A Black nursery nurse working in one of the nursery units confirmed this:

> They (the White teachers) have got this way of talking to them (Asian children) in a really simple way ... cutting half the sentences 'Me no do that' sort of thing ... and that is not standard English. And they've [teachers] got this way of saying words 'That naughty' and they miss words out and it really does seem stupid ... I feel that it's not my place to say 'Well that's a silly way to speak to children ...' I worry about what it tells the white children who think that the Asian children are odd anyway.

Not all educators appreciate that Creole is a language in its own right. They may not know that slaves in the Caribbean were prohibited from speaking their own languages and that Creole gradually developed from the various African languages to become a common language. Children from African-Caribbean families who are currently learning English as an additional language in nurseries/schools need to have their learning supported, praised, encouraged and carefully monitored. The Rampton Report (1981:23) drew attention to the importance of acknowledging Creole as a language:

> The attitude of schools and teachers towards a West Indian child's home language is of critical importance. If teachers simply reject a West Indian child's language as 'bad English' the child may see the rejection as meaning that he is inadequate and that his family and indeed his ethnic group are not respected by the teachers.

## Learning by doing

Both Black children and White whose home language is English vary in their ability to use and understand it. Educators use a range of strategies and provide opportunities for them to ask questions, talk to each other, and 'play' with language. This means that what is already happening in many early years settings provides the groundwork on which the support for children who are learning English as an additional language can be built. Children can be encouraged to share their language experiences in a sensitive and respectful way and their ability to use more than one language acknowledged and praised. For example, an enjoyable learning experience might be to invite all the children to say what they call members of their family, to share other ways of saying words and phrases like hello, how are you, goodbye, I'm feeling happy/sad or I'm hungry. They could find out whether words like please, yes, no, are used in the same way in all languages and whether there are different 'rules' when people speak to each other, e.g. are they taught to look directly at the person who is speaking to them or would this be considered rude, especially if the person was somebody in authority like a teacher or somebody older than themselves?

Children benefit from a curriculum which acknowledges and promotes the cultural and linguistic heritage of every child and enables all of them to understand, speak, read and write in English while promoting respect for languages other than their own. It provides opportunities for the skills, needs and learning styles of each to be developed, encourages the expression of creative, cognitive and linguistic skills in their home language and/or in English.

Having texts from a range of cultures not only supports children for whom English is an additional language but also enhances all children's communication skills and motivates them to use and learn a variety of languages.

'Can Do' books and 'Records of Achievement' can acknowledge the languages that each child is learning and using. Bilingual and multilingual children can experience the satisfaction of having their skills appreciated and their languages valued. They can feel comfortable speaking their own language and good about being able to share it with the other children. Parents, and especially Black parents, are likely to be motivated to provide relevant information and opportunities to participate in resourcing and decision making.

Before they start nursery/school the majority of young British children who are learning English as an additional language have been exposed to English through the television, hearing their friends, siblings or their parents speaking English, and on outings such as shopping and going to the doctor. Newcomers to Britain may not have had much experience of hearing English and may require extra support.

Black children are sometimes treated as if they are a homogeneous group – which is not the case. As Edwards (1995) notes, Panjabi Sikhs and Muslims, for example, have been in Britain since the 1950s while others like the Somalis and the Tamils arrived more recently, fleeing for their lives from their home countries. There are also class differences within linguistic communities. For instance, those Panjabi speakers who arrived via East Africa tend to come from middle class backgrounds and have a high level of education while those from India and Pakistan have tended to come from rural backgrounds with little formal education. Many families from linguistic minority communities speak English at home so their children will be fluent English speakers when they come to nursery/school. Each child has her/his own individual needs and experiences which influence her/his learning.

Even in areas where English is the home language of all the children, we need to find out which languages other than English are spoken by the local population and include these in our provision to enhance children's communication skills and awaken their interest and motivation to learn languages different from their own. White parents from minority ethnic communities who speak, for instance, Yiddish, Polish or Gaelic may need to be encouraged to reveal this skill.

Young children come into group settings able to use language in many different ways and to learn through it. For a variety of reasons, some children experience language delay – perhaps because they are hearing impaired. Delay can be missed when the children are learning English as an additional language because we may attribute their lack of progress to the fact that their home language is not English so overlook other possible causes. It is crucial to identify these children and to give them appropriate support.

## Bilingual support

Having bilingual assistants who speak a range of community languages in the nursery/school and are able to support monolingual educators has obvious advantages. By communicating in children's home languages, tapping into their cultural and linguistic knowledge, they help children feel more secure and confident and able to join in and learn. Their presence can relax parents and encourage their active participation. Monolingual children can see languages other than English being valued and respected. A Chinese bilingual assistant describes an incident in the family centre in which she works:

> Suyuan who is Chinese and her English-speaking friend Amanda had obviously enjoyed the experience of eating together in a Chinese restaurant. They decided to open one of their own. They spent a great deal of time carefully setting it up with appropriate table-cloths, bowls and chopsticks from the home corner. I helped them make flowers for the tables and agreed to write the menu in Chinese. The two girls dressed up as cooks. I was to be the waitress. When the other children and the teacher came for a meal, I helped them to read the menu and decide what they wanted to order. The children behaved in a respectful way and seemed to thoroughly enjoy 'going out for dinner'. To Suyuan's and Amanda's delight the teacher asked if she could meet the cooks because the meal had been so delicious!

Bilingual students also make a valuable contribution, especially if educators have large classes and have little time or patience to respond to children who are learning English as an additional language. This incident was recounted by a student teacher:

> Several weeks into the term a parent who had just moved into the neighbourhood brought her Urdu-speaking little boy into the room, introduced him to the teacher and quickly left. The teacher smiled pleasantly, showed him where to sit, put some crayons and paper on the table and told him that the children were drawing pictures of their mothers. The little boy burst into tears.
>
> The teacher said, 'No, no. Don't cry'. I moved closer to comfort him but the teacher waved me away.
>
> She said sternly: 'Leave him alone or he'll be crying till June'. She returned to the group of children with whom she had been working.
>
> I tried ignoring him but his crying was too pitiful. I sat down next to him and gently stroked his back. He put his head on the table and sobbed.
>
> I whispered in Urdu: 'You want your mummy?' He stared at me with tear-filled eyes and nodded.

I said: 'She'll come back soon and then you can go home. In the meantime should we make a picture of your mummy?'

Another nod. He gradually stopped crying and watched as I drew a circle for the face. I asked: 'Do you want to draw her eyes?'

He picked up a crayon and carefully made two little circles, added a line for the nose and was soon absorbed in his drawing.

In nurseries/schools where children speak a wide range of languages it is not possible to employ bilingual staff to provide language support for all these different language speakers. The 'problem' can be solved by drawing on the expertise of bilingual parents. They are invited to come in and help by reading and/or telling stories to the children, providing explanations and helping concept-building during, for instance, cooking and science activities. Although their contribution is extremely valuable, it would seem that a more logical and far-reaching solution would be if their initial training provided all students with the attitudes, skills and knowledge they need for supporting and teaching children who are learning English as an additional language.

Children who are hearing impaired and who are learning English as an additional language are not very likely to have access to a bilingual assistant who can sign in their home languages. However, British Sign Language can be learnt and will provide these children with access to English as an additional language and to the National Curriculum. It also gives hearing children access to the deaf community, to deaf culture and the opportunity to explore a living language and learn a skill that could stay with them for the rest of their lives.

Many bilingual assistants find their job stressful because they tend to lack training, especially on bilingual issues, their posts carry little status and some members of staff are hostile and patronising. Extra pressure may come from having to act as interpreters with no extra time allocated for this additional work or from feeling that their skills are unacknowledged and unvalued. They may also be expected to produce story cassettes and write notices in their home languages, which may be a problem for those who do not read and write in their home languages. Marilyn Martin-Jones and Mukul Saxena (1996) found that an unequal power relationship often existed between bilingual assistants and monolingual teachers. Consequently, many teachers unwittingly undermined the authority and self-esteem of the assistants. Martin-Jones and Saxena claim that children are not only aware of this but also conclude that English must be the more important language because it is the language used by the teacher and she/he has the greater power and status within the classroom. Trying to create a more equal relationship between bilingual assistants and educators is a challenging and important task. Changing the title from assistant to, for example, consultant might help to shift the balance. The suggestions offered by Louise Derman-Sparks and Carol Brunson Phillips (1997:144) not only apply to the working relationship between educators and their bilingual assistants but to all situations in which people are working together:

> All team teaching situations require careful attention to how power is shared. Ongoing communication, negotiation, and evaluation are essential. Interracial team teaching carries an added responsibility – paying attention to the social as well as the personal meanings of behaviour. ... Another interaction to watch for is White teachers always having the last word. Unconscious racist interactions will inevitably occur since (educators) ... do not escape the conditioning of a racist society. Accordingly, regular, critical and honest discussion of the team's interactions is required regardless of how small a particular issue seems. ... Moreover, the different teaching strengths, skills and styles that each teacher brings to the group must be honoured but not used as an excuse for an imbalance of power.

We should not assume that once children are conversationally fluent in English, they require no further support. Even after they have achieved conversational fluency it can take from five to seven years to catch up academically. Conversational language is supported by various cues such as gestures, intonation and facial expressions but academic language provides no such cues. So these children need continued support to help them catch up with their classmates whose home language is English. If they don't receive support through their home languages many work with one hand tied behind their backs. Rose Drury (1997:34) describes nine year old Naseem who has been in the school since she joined the nursery class. She communicates with her classmates in English but her command of it is not sufficient for school learning and she is struggling with the demands of the curriculum:

The session starts with a whole class discussion about geography work on the British Isles. Naseem sits with a group of friends, passive and disengaged. The class then return to their desks and continue the ongoing classwork which was introduced earlier in the week. ... Most of the children in the class are working in small groups but Naseem in sitting on her own. ... During the session she is easily distracted and off task for most of the time. ... it is evident that the question 'how many times bigger than Northern Ireland is the Republic of Ireland?' is difficult for her to understand. She sits at her desk with her hand up, asking for help. After several minutes the class teacher asks the class to tidy up.

## Practical strategies

Although general teaching strategies can be effectively used, learning English as an additional language is a complex process requiring considerable input. Edwards (1995) compares this process through which children are consolidating their home language while learning the new language to learning to play a musical instrument, because it takes time, encouragement, practice and needs to be accompanied by feelings of success. Children can remain silent for weeks or months at nursery/school while continuing to speak to their families in their own language. They are acquiring knowledge of English and when they are ready and confident enough, they will start speaking it. During the silent phase children listen and watch and perhaps respond in their first language or through gestures and actions.

Research by Tizard and Hughes (1984) indicates that children learn language best when they talk with adults about things that interest them, rather than being specifically taught particular words and phrases or being asked questions. The children may not understand the words being used but they will understand eye contact, smiles and reassuring touches. Once they feel safe and have built a sense of trust, they are ready to interact and communicate. The fact that children have to talk in order to learn a language means that we need to give them language practising opportunities. We may believe that it is helpful for new children to spend much of the day playing quietly on their own but this will not support their learning of an additional language.

Children learning English as an additional language learn best when they:

* are encouraged to participate in a wide range of activities that stimulate communication in an environment which reflects their own cultural and linguistic background. Games are especially helpful because they can participate fully by using words and body language. When games are also provided in the children's home languages, confidence and skills can be developed which can, in turn, contribute to the learning of English.

* are exposed to language which is appropriate to their level of development, which is meaningful, based on concrete experiences and supported by visual and concrete experiences. They make most progress when the focus is on meaning and not on words and grammar. Their understanding is boosted by using short sentences, giving them directions one at a time, talking to them as though they understand and then illustrating the meaning by involving them in appropriate action.

* are involved in practical activities because young children learn best from hands on experiences.

* feel secure and esteemed in a supportive environment. What children can do is built on and celebrated.

* are encouraged and not continually corrected. Mistakes are part of the process of learning to speak a language. Iram Siraj-Blatchford (1994:54) notes mistakes may stem from the structure of their home languages:

> Children whose first language is Hindi, Urdu or Panjabi may be heard making similar mistakes such as, 'I will shut door.' It is not surprising that they omit the article (in this case 'the'), before words such as door, because as a direct translation from the home language it makes sense – most South Asian languages do not use articles.

- have educators who quickly learn the names that are unfamiliar to them and pronounce them the way the parents do and have learned some words in the children's home languages.

The languages children speak, their sense of identity and their self-esteem are all closely bound together. When we view children able to speak languages other than English as having a special skill and support them by incorporating their languages into the curriculum, we are also broadening the horizons of monolingual children whose home language is English. In addition, we are helping to dispel the myth that English is superior to other languages and that those who are fluent in it are also superior. By encouraging children to be proud of their home languages we are helping to prevent the pain experienced by many families when their children are ashamed to speak them. Encouraging pride in children's rich linguistic heritage can also help to ensure that their language(s) do not die out as happened, for example, to some Aboriginal and Native American languages and could happen to Gaelic and Yiddish.

For us as educators good communication involves respect, the ability to express oneself clearly, to understand and empathise with people, to be willing and able to try to resolve conflicts and to compromise. These skills are particularly useful if parents are proficient in a range of languages and we can only speak English.

# Chapter 5
# Old enough to decide?

*... we wish to aid the development of our most precious natural resource: the minds and hearts of our children and young people. It is their curiosity, their eagerness to learn, their ability to make difficult and complex choices that will decide the future of our world.* Rogers and Freiberg

We can only know about the misinformation and misunderstandings that children have absorbed if we provide opportunities for them to say what they think about discriminatory issues. This chapter discusses some of the strategies and activities already in use to encourage children to express their thoughts and feelings about inequalities, to make up their own minds about what they feel is fair and to encourage them to work collaboratively. It suggests how we can build on such good practice.

Children are powerful thinkers and learners. Vygotsky (1978) proposed that they acquire the tools they need by interacting with people who know more than they do. By being sensitive to young children's intentions and meanings we can provide a framework, a 'scaffold' for promoting learning – stimulating them to express their thoughts and feelings. Enabling children to share their ideas and experiences in this way is something that we do all the time although not all of us create environments to encourage children to express what they honestly feel about how they are treated and the way they treat others. Given the opportunity, children are able to think about equality issues and make up their own minds about what they feel is fair and just. This has been demonstrated over and over again. Yet there is still a view that although it is a good idea for children to be encouraged to talk and think about discriminatory issues, it is not for us as educators to present them with alternative views because 'children bring their beliefs from home'. Do we have the same problem intervening when children bring guns and other war toys to the nursery/school from home or when girls are not able to play freely because they might dirty their pretty dresses or scuff their patent leather shoes?

Piaget's theory that young children are egocentric and therefore not able to decentre has been used to support the claim that raising issues of discrimination with them is inappropriate because they have not yet reached the stage when they are able to think about people and situations other than their own. Distinguished developmental psychologists such as Margaret Donaldson (1978) strongly disagree with Piaget. She claims that the tasks and problems on which he based his theory were unrelated to children's own knowledge and experience. She showed that young children performed far better on tasks that related to what they already knew and which were embedded in an appropriate context than they did on the tasks set by Piaget. The ability to decentre is dependant not on children's developmental stage but on how tasks are presented to them. Judy Dunn (1993:109) agrees that young children are capable of decentring:

> Most children recognise and respond to the feeling of others and behave practically to improve or worsen other people's emotional state. They understand the connections between others' beliefs and desires, and their behaviour. They have some grasp of what is appropriate moral behaviour for different relationships. Such sophistication means that even young children can be supportive, concerned, intimate and humorous with others – or they can be manipulative, devious and teasing and deliberately upset others.

In chapter three I discussed the notion that children are innocent and unaware of harsh realities like racism and that their innocence is violated and conflict intensified when they are encouraged to explore and discuss equality issues. But for large numbers of children the world is full of harsh realities and complex relationships and even children whose own lives are happy and secure are aware of and influenced by the injustice and discrimination that operates outside their immediate environment.

## Equality matters

Raising equality issues with young children can arouse fears of indoctrination. These fears could be valid if the issues are raised in an authoritarian way, i.e. if the educator tells children what they should think. But if children are encouraged to discuss their ideas freely and make up their own minds, their knowledge base and their horizons are likely to be widened. One can argue that children are being indoctrinated when nurseries/schools uncritically reflect the dominant values and beliefs of society and children are being continually exposed to these values and beliefs through the overt and hidden curriculum. If this is indeed what happens, children could grow up assuming that the way society is organised is the way it has to be and that it cannot be changed. Cummins (1996a:11) asks:

> Are we preparing pupils to accept the societal status quo (and, in many cases, their own inferior status therein) or are we preparing them to participate actively and critically in the democratic process in pursuit of the ideals of social justice and equity that are enshrined in the constitutions of most countries around the world?

The National Curriculum Council's Guidance on Citizenship (1990) recommends that children should learn about civil, political, social and human rights and how various forms of injustice, inequality and discrimination, including sexism and racism, are violated. Although this recommendation refers to older children, it can equally be applied to younger ones who learn about and use the concept of 'fairness' in their daily lives. 'It's not fair!' is a familiar cry loudly proclaimed. So it is surely developmentally appropriate to encourage, support, and extend children's understanding and help them develop strategies and confidence to deal with unfair situations and to realise that they can bring about change. Louise Derman-Sparks (1993:17) indicates how children's sense of fairness can spur them to act:

In a school for children with special needs there was no parking space in the teacher's car park allocated to people with disabilities. One year a parent who used a wheelchair couldn't come to an open evening because she was not able to park close enough to the school. When this was discussed with the children they readily saw that it wasn't fair. They went on a trip to look at various kinds of parking, came back to the school and created a special parking place for people with disabilities. It so happened that their classroom overlooked the car park so they could see if teachers were parking 'fairly' or not. Some weren't, so the children designed tickets and, being too young to write, dictated what they wanted to say. They gave tickets to those who parked in the place designated for a disabled driver. The children were gratified to see that the teachers then parked 'fairly'.

And, at a family centre:

The teacher showed a group of children a box of plasters and told them, 'The plasters in this box are called flesh coloured, which means that they match our skin. Let us do a test to see if they do'. Each child proceeded to put a plaster on her/his skin and ticked a chart according to whether it matched or not. They then extended their investigation by testing the plasters out on other children in the Centre and on their parents. After discussing their findings with the teacher, the children decided that as the plasters didn't match everybody's skin, it was not fair to call them flesh coloured. Their next step was to dictate a letter for their teacher to send to the company. Back came a letter with two boxes of transparent plasters. The children thought that these were much better than the 'flesh coloured' ones.

Clearly then, even young children are able to consider issues, think about the consequences and offer alternative solutions. It is our responsibility as educators to provide appropriate opportunities and encouragement to find out what children think, value their opinions and uncover any misconceptions they may have acquired. This is vital because these influence the way children interpret new information presented to them. An educator may have excellent material about, for instance, Travellers but if the children have absorbed misinformation about this group, they will incorporate the new information into their existing beliefs.

## Collaborative approaches

Anti-discriminatory practice and collaborative learning go hand in hand. How we encourage children to learn is as important as, and inseparable from, the content of what they learn. Active collaborative learning in small groups can promote the development of concepts, skills, attitudes and the ability to argue rationally. It is a challenging approach which does not fit easily with a curriculum geared to compartmentalised knowledge, back to basics and formal teaching methods. It requires instead that we equip children with the understanding and skills they need to pass on information, share ideas, ask questions, make up their own minds about what they feel is fair and just and empower them to stand up for themselves and others when they encounter discrimination. Collaborative learning promotes understanding and encourages boys and girls of different cultures and abilities to consider and talk about equality issues and to carry out awareness raising tasks together. During this process educators are active participants, supporting and guiding learning appropriately.

Encouraging children to work and play collaboratively requires more than simply giving a task to a small group and telling them to get on with it. The completion of the task must involve them in working together and, in the process, recognising and respecting their own skill and knowledge and that of the other children in the group. Working and playing together like this gives them the chance to experience co-operation and conflict, power and inequality, similarities and differences. It can help children to recognise the individuality of others and thus contribute to breaking down stereotypes and prejudices. And it can enable less confident children to express themselves. The emphasis is shifted away from individual competitive learning and away from the power and authority of the adult on to the children as active co-operative learners and problem solvers who feel a sense of ownership and belonging.

To prevent the voices of the more articulate and self-assured drowning the others the groups need to be carefully planned. Skelton (1988) highlights research by Tann (1981) that showed how girls avoid challenging each other – although there are exceptions – whereas boys in a mixed group tend to take risks and be more dynamic. Edwards (1995) points out that boys in mixed groups tend to talk more than girls, interrupt more and be more aggressive. Girls on the other hand tend to defer to other people's ideas and offer encouragement and support for other speakers in the group. Games in which children have to co-operate to play and which promote turn-taking can help develop social skills, a greater sense of belonging and confidence to participate in other activities.

Establish ground rules and review them periodically to ensure that everyone in the group is clear about the responsibilities they have towards each other. Expressing these rules as do's instead of dont's is likely to have more effect and help to create an appropriate setting. Rules could include telling the truth, listening to each other, showing respect, caring for each other's feelings. A useful small group activity could be defining what each rule means and asking what would need to be done to ensure that the rules are implemented – questions like: what would we need to do to make sure that everyone is listened to? In some nurseries/schools a 'talking' object is passed around so that only the child who has the object in her/his hand can speak – though nobody has to talk if they don't want to.

Creating opportunities to work on equality issues requires us to be sensitive and encouraging, willing to listen, hear and respond while at the same time, never ignoring the possible impact on other children in the group of what is being said. We must take care not to encourage stereotypical thinking nor assume that because children share a culture they also share the same views, beliefs, values and attitudes.

We need to be especially sensitive to the feelings of children from Black, refugee, Traveller, lesbian or gay families and children with learning difficulties or physical impairments. It is quite possible that children will express very negative views when encouraged to talk about their feelings and attitudes. Have some possible responses ready, and if necessary consult colleagues and parents.

Black children in predominantly White groups might not wish to make themselves vulnerable by discussing their experiences of racism with White educators and children and they should not be put on the spot. Too often, children from oppressed groups are expected to bear the burden of explaining their experiences to those from the dominant group. If they remain silent their feelings should be respected and supported. It is unethical to put children into a situation which might be upsetting for them.

Cultural differences exist in the body language that children learn from an early age and we may be unaware of some of them. Many White children are taught to look directly at an adult to whom they are speaking or when they are being spoken to, for example. If they don't, it is generally assumed that they aren't listening or that they feel guilty about something they've done. But many Black children are taught that to keep their eyes lowered shows respect.

Children are more likely to feel comfortable about exploring equality issues if they feel that we really care about what they do and say. Trust has to be built up between us and the children as well as among the children themselves so that everyone's feelings and opinions are respected and valued. The aim is to promote self-esteem, assertiveness, confidence and empathy.

## Circle times

As educators of young children we are very familiar with circle time – sitting with the children so that we all have eye contact with one another because, as Mosely (1993) says: '*the circle is a symbol of unity, wholeness and harmony*'. We can trigger discussion around equality issues, uncover negative attitudes and beliefs which might otherwise remain unexpressed and unchallenged, and we can enable children to see themselves as being active players in the struggle for change. Events in the community or in the neighbourhood of the nursery/school or that have been presented on television can be used to spark discussion. This may seem an obvious thing to do but we do not usually discuss, for example, local or national demonstrations with the children. Everyone needs to feel safe, able to reflect on their own feelings and reactions and to develop empathy.

# REGULAR CIRCLE-TIME HELPS YOUR SCHOOL AND YOUR PUPILS

© Jenny Mosley
© Illustration Simon Barnes

Children's questions can present educators with 'teachable moments' which can be used to encourage children to express their feelings and views. For example, a five year old girl in America asked, 'If Columbus was mean and cruel to the Indians, why do we celebrate Columbus Day?' During the ensuing discussion the teacher encouraged the children in the class to think about the issues. They came to the conclusion that '*it would be better to have Native American's Day instead*'. In a nursery school a member of staff overheard a child asking his friend about a new child in the group who was learning English as an additional language: 'Why can't that girl talk?' The next circle time was used to talk about the holidays that children had been on. The teacher asked them whether the people in the countries they visited spoke languages other than English and how the children felt when they were not able to understand what was being said.

Giving accurate information and encouraging children to ask questions and express their views and feelings helps children to think again about their ideas. They might, for example, think that wheelchair users can't do anything for themselves. If they look at and discuss a picture of an adult in a wheelchair they can begin to think about the things the person could do. The next step would be to think about how everybody, abled and disabled adults and children, uses aids and needs people to help them. Children could be encouraged to talk about all the aids they use and the way people help them from when they get up in the morning till the time they come into nursery/school.

Circle time can be followed with creative activities and tasks done in small collaborative groups that will deepen children's understanding of the issues and encourage the expression of feelings.

X **Questions, questions, questions**
Skilful questioning fosters children's self esteem and ensures that the rest of the group values their contributions. This is how the teacher in this incident described by Faber and Mazlish (1996:190) responded to Charlene, a little girl who finds learning difficult.

> Charlene put up her hand during a story about a bee keeper and asked, 'Do a bee be a bird?'.

The rest of the children were electrified. Several raised their hands and eagerly waved them about. The teacher said, 'Wait a minute children. Charlene, that is such an interesting question! What makes you think a bee could be a bird?'

Very solemnly Charlene replied, 'They both got wings.'

'Is there anything else the same?'

'They fly.'

'You noticed two things that were the same. Class, is there anything that makes birds different from bees?'

'Birds got feathers.'

'Birds is bigger.'

'Birds don't sting you.'

Suddenly Charlene's face lit up.

'I know, I know,' she called out. 'A bee is an INCEST!'

All the heads nodded.

On the board the teacher wrote the children's conclusion: 'A bee is an insect.'

How we ask questions and the kind of questions we ask is significant. Questioning children elicits information and encourages children to think about issues but the act of asking, particularly closed questions, may increase adults' power and reduce children's spontaneity and willingness to express their true feelings and views. Over-directive behaviour may result in children seeing themselves and being seen by other children as less competent. Wood and Wood found that teachers tended to dominate in classrooms, asked questions of a testing nature and didn't give children enough chance to answer. They concluded that the person who questions is in control and the person answering runs the risk of being considered ignorant. A study by Ogilvy and others (1992) which was part of a broader investigation into adult/child interaction styles in eight multi-ethnic nursery schools, found that the teachers had a more controlling style when relating to the Asian children. White Scottish children were asked many questions, but the Asian children were asked significantly more. The researchers claim that the number of questions and the way the teachers asked them put the Asian children under pressure.

Questions that place children in the role of 'experts' however, help to uncover their beliefs and stereotypical thinking and encourage them to think about their own assumptions. Questions like:

How do you know that you are a girl/boy?

Do you think that a girl is someone with long hair? What about .....? He is a boy and he has long hair.

Do you think that a boy is someone who is strong? What about ......? She is a girl and she is strong.

Do you think that all girls are frightened of spiders? How do you know?

Do you think that women are very good at fixing cars and machines? How do you know?

Do you think that boys shouldn't cry? How do you know?

Do you think that all children live in houses with their mums and dads? How do you know?

Do you think everybody eats fish and chips? How do you know?

 The following activity is adapted from a task developed with older children by Brown and others (1991:35). It is designed to deepen children's awareness of their own feelings and those of other people:

> Children in a first year infant classroom selected two sheets of paper they considered most closely matched the colour of their skin. They were then asked to draw a happy face on one piece of paper, a sad face on the other and to paste a spatula onto the back of each. They were encouraged to talk about their drawings with the other children on their table while they did so. After completing this task they sat in a circle with the educator. She told them that she was going to ask them some questions that they could answer by holding up the drawing that described how they felt. Questions like:

How do you feel if somebody smiles at you?

How do you feel if somebody pushes you?

How do you feel if somebody tells you that they like you?

How do you feel when somebody calls you names?

The educator encouraged them to talk about some of their choices. The children then took turns asking the questions and the educator joined in with her own pictures of faces.

## Books

Suggesting to educators that they should use books is like telling builders to use bricks. But do we encourage young children to identify with the characters in them who have been treated unfairly? Do we provide books in which the central characters are powerful Black adults and children, Travellers, refugees, girls and boys, disabled adults and children, gays and lesbians? Through the stories we tell and the books we offer we enable children to learn about the world, share and pass on their own cultural traditions, recognise and challenge stereotypes and enjoy the experience of being part of a creative and stimulating group activity. This is important for children whose communities or countries of origin are traditionally viewed in a negative way and for those children who have absorbed prevailing negative views. Books like *A is for Africa* by Ifeoma Onyefulu (1993) and *I is for India* by Prodeepta Das (1996) present very positive images of the countries featured.

There are books that confront important issues sensitively and appropriately for young children. *The Boy Who Wouldn't Speak* by Steve Barry (1989) tells the story of Owen, who befriends the two giants who have moved into his road. A campaign is launched to make them move away. Only when he needs to defend his two friends does Owen speak.

*Racism* by Angela Grunsell (!990) is a thoughtful, sensitive exploration of issues relevant to all children. *Black Like Kyra, White Like Me* by Judith Vigna (1989) describes the racism that Kyra and her family meet when they move into a White neighbourhood.

Encouraging children to talk about books like these can help them empathise with the characters who are treated unfairly and uncover any stereotypical attitudes and negative beliefs they have picked up. Ask them questions such as:

Why would you want or not want to have a friend like ........? (characters in the story)

What do you like (not like) about the way the story ends?

What do you like (not like) about the illustrations?

How did the story make you feel?

There are books like *The Patchwork Quilt* by Valerie Flournoy (1985) or *A Chair for my Mother* by Vera B. Williams (1982) which can stimulate discussion about mothers, aunts and grandmothers. In these stories housewives and mothers are portrayed as strong, independent, warm and loving women. Sue Adler (1993:113) calls these feminist books and explains that:

> Feminism examines power relations, mainly (though not exclu-sively) between the sexes. In children's books, as in other areas of study, it is not an ideology of sexual differences that is at issue; it is assumptions about male superiority and female inferiority and the abuse of power that should be under scrutiny. Feminism is not only concerned with the struggle for political and economic change but also with valuing women's experience, with notions (however idealistic) of sisterhood, and therefore with challenges to patriarchy.

Some books are anti-sexist, antiracist or both, have positive images of disabled people and of men doing domestic chores, but continue to perpetuate the idea that all families consist of a mother, father and their children, usually a boy and a girl. Children whose experience of family is different from this ideal may feel that theirs is of less value and, perhaps, something to be ashamed about. These feelings may be re-inforced by the attitudes of children who live in more traditional families. We can try to broaden the attitudes of these children and help support children from non-traditional families by reading and talking about books that show different forms of family life. *Through My Window* by Tony Bradman and Eileen Browne (1988) and *Billy and*

*Belle* by Sarah Garland (1993) are about mixed parentage families and *My Mom is so Unusual* by Iris Loewen (1986) is one of many delightful tales about a single parent family. *Snowy* by Berlie Doherty (1992) features a Traveller family. Discussions about the similarities and differences in family routines and practices, meal times, going to bed, what usually happens at the weekend, and on birthdays can help children appreciate that there are lots of different, but equally valid ways of living in a family. With infant school children discussions could be linked to Key Stage 1 History – Claire (1996) explores possibilities for extending children's perspective on the past and the present.

Working from an anti-discriminatory perspective requires that books are carefully selected. Others that clearly exclude certain groups or portray them negatively can be used to raise awareness of prejudice, discrimination and stereotyping.

## Persona dolls

These are special dolls we use to tell stories that raise equality issues and encourage the sharing of thoughts and feelings. To enable the children to bond and identify with them, give each persona doll her/his own name, personality, family and life history and build up a range representing adults and children from diverse backgrounds, especially those in the nursery/school. Displaying their photographs in appropriate parts of the room encourages the children to think of the dolls as part of the group. Parents can be asked to help make the dolls and their clothes, especially if there is a child at the nursery/school with, let us say, a particular disability and the appropriate doll is not commercially manufactured. Parent involvement ensures that the dolls and their clothes are culturally appropriate and that physical features are accurately portrayed.

Once they have been introduced to the children, stories can be woven around the dolls for the rest of the year. One could be told about a particular doll – let's call her Beverley. She is four years old, loves riding her bike, painting and looking at books. She can't hear very well so everyone in her family uses sign language when they talk to her. Sometimes children tease her and then she feels sad. She lives with her Black mum who is a doctor, her White dad who is a nursery school teacher, her sisters, Pam who is 7 and Irene who is 9 years old. They live in a flat which is right next to a park. Beverley has just started going to the same school as her sisters. ... The children can be encouraged to tell their own stories about the dolls and their families.

## Pictures

By listening to what children say about the pictures we select, we can get an idea of how they see the world and may well find evidence of misinformation, stereotypical judgements and assumptions. Debbie Epstein (1993) describes how using photographs with children in a reception class triggered a discussion on name-calling and what it felt like to be called names. Two of the boys expressed dislike of Black people and were challenged by other children. A little girl asked them: 'How can you not like people you don't know?'

Ross and Browne (1993) suggest taking photographs of various areas and equipment in the nursery/school (with no children present) to explore children's perceptions of the gender roles of boys and girls. Children can be shown the photographs and asked which areas and equipment they like playing with most and which they like least – encouraging them to give their reasons.

## Drama and video

Drama and role-playing can also highlight fair and unfair situations, cultural similarities and differences and they give children opportunities to express their feelings in a safe setting. If children are initially reluctant to take part an educator may have to assume one of the roles. Finding out what it feels like to be in someone else's shoes encourages empathy and can stimulate lively discussion. A creative way to develop critical awareness is to dramatise stories that raise equality issues and encourage children to act out alternative story lines or endings. If a video-camera is available, events, activities and interactions in the nursery/school can be recorded and shown to the children. This has been found to help them see how they relate to one another and encourage them to respond to unfair situations. A video made of play in a nursery class and shown to the children caused one little boy to comment, 'Nicola looks sad' and another to say, 'Next time I'll ask her to play with me'.

Troyna and Hatcher (1992) in their study of mainly White primary schools stress that although racism is prevalent, children also have a strong egalitarian sense on which we can build. In many nursery/ schools children are happily talking about what they think while their educators are able to support and guide them without restricting their capacity to contribute ideas. Open-ended, collaborative and experiential learning opportunities are enabling the children to free themselves as much as possible from discriminatory attitudes, heightening their concept of fairness and empowering them to actively challenge discrimination.

## Chapter 6
# Building Bridges

*'I learn everything I want to know from my mum, I learn everything I don't want to know in school.'* A six year old child

Collaborative relationships between educators and parents need to be based on mutual trust and respect and built within an anti-discriminatory framework This involves identifying the beliefs, attitudes and assumptions which may consciously or unconsciously be affecting collaboration and understanding the structural barriers – such as racism – which may influence parents' participation. This chapter outlines some ideas for creating an environment where all parents can feel that they belong and are valued.

The Children Act (1989) and the Guidance and Regulations Vol 2 stress the importance of developing partnerships with parents and appreciating that parents have rights and responsibility for their children. When educators support each other, look for the best in each other and acknowledge one another's efforts, we are well placed to work closely together with parents and give of our best to the children. Providing a network of support for parents fosters personal growth, develops confidence and self-esteem. For many parents it is the first time that they are handing their children over to strangers. They may be feeling vulnerable so initial contacts need to be friendly and supportive and the atmosphere relaxed and welcoming.

Working closely with parents is an integral part of an anti-discriminatory approach. It is creative and rewarding but it is a complex process that can be difficult to implement. Many nurseries/schools are forging close links with parents and successfully involving and empowering them. But even here, parents tend to be junior partners – there is a deeply rooted unequal power relationship between staff who are professionals and parents who are not. It is quite possible that educators, especially when newly qualified or with fewer paper qualifications, do not see themselves as powerful people, yet to parents they represent the establishment. As educators our power is especially apparent in infant schools where we have the ultimate responsibility for drawing up a curriculum that is in line with concepts like discovery learning and learning readiness. It is we who create an environment that supports appropriate learning opportunities to match the children's stage of development. Parents do not generally have knowledge, expertise or skills of this nature. Even in settings for younger children where parents may be more involved in planning and making decisions, they do not have our power, authority or control. They make an important contribution but do so as our assistants. Having greater power gives us ultimate responsibility for establishing and developing collaborative relationships with parents. As Iram Siraj-Blatchford (1994:95) observes:

> For parents to participate in the daily life of an early years setting there must be real and obvious commitment from staff. It is not enough to use the rhetoric of parents as 'partners' in the education of their children. ... In the process of providing information and establishing a partnership it is staff who must take the lead responsibility – they are the ones with the power.

This responsibility requires that we try to understand the personal and social reasons why some parents are less able to become involved. Parents who participate regularly have more opportunities to express their opinions and feelings, be listened to and have their ideas acted upon. Middle class parents tend to be disproportionately more involved – many employ people to help them at home. They tend to feel more confident with us, and they know how the education system works.

Parents who have gone through the British education system success-fully are more likely to feel comfortable about their role and confident about offering their skills and knowledge whereas those who feel un-happy about their own schooling might feel that they don't have much to contribute to their children's learning. Some parents may have had scant experience of schooling in their country of birth and feel un-comfortable about even coming into the nursery/school, never mind being involved in it.

Nurseries/schools are not all equally committed to building partner-ships. In some, parents may receive plenty of encouragement and opportunities to contribute while in others their contribution may be restricted to fund-raising. Building collaborative relationships is generally conceived with mothers not fathers in mind, even though women are increasingly in work and men are increasingly facing un-employment. Mothers who are at home are generally assumed to be free, able and willing to participate. For some, the time that their chil-dren are at school may be the only time they have to undertake training or to develop their own interests. For many, meeting the domestic and economic needs of their family leaves them little time or energy to devote to the nursery/school.

For collaboration to be effective the child rearing practices of parents need to be valued and respected and the parents actively involved in the caring and education of their children. Pre-conceived ideas about parents may cause us to stereotype and devalue their skills and know-ledge. We may believe that 'professionals know best' and feel that some parents are not providing their children with the 'right' kind of stimulation and play experiences to enable them to come to nursery/school ready to learn. Working mothers may receive the message that they are failing in their parenting role because they can't spend time with their children at nursery/school. If we believe that there is only one 'right' way to bring up children – the way we were brought up – we are likely to view parents whose child rearing patterns are different from ours as inadequate and disinterested.

Staff cuts, fewer resources and more and more paperwork can lead to a situation where parents perceive us as inflexible and unapproachable, too absorbed with our busy routine to deal with their needs and enable them to contribute. This can deter some parents from becoming involved and prevent others from making a long term commitment. Pressures restrict the time and energy staff have to meet and plan with parents. Feeling already over-burdened, some staff may resent this extra workload and may feel that having to keep parents feeling useful takes time away from the children.

As educators receive scant training about how to work effectively with parents, we may find having them in the room threatening and undermining. This is especially likely if the parents are mature and confident and we are newly qualified. Some of us feel that our professional status is particularly threatened by middle class parents who know their rights and insist upon them. Or we may think that middle class parents are particularly useful because they are in tune with our own expectations of the children and we perceive them as being actively involved in their children's learning. We may consider that working alongside parents who have a physical disability is more of a hindrance than a help and be concerned about the safety not only of the adults but also of the children.

Relationships are unlikely to be collaborative if we interpret assertiveness by parents, especially Black or working class parents, as aggression, or if we express – or indeed hold – stereotyped opinions about ethnic, cultural, or religious groups. One staff member was heard to say:

> You'd think that being the only Jewish child in the school, David would try and fit in especially as he doesn't even look Jewish. But he just keeps himself to himself, you know the way they do. You hardly notice him. Mind you, he certainly doesn't take after his parents. They are so incredibly pushy. Mark my words, in no time they'll be taking over the school.

## Parents' perspectives

Parents are individuals with different needs, skills, fears and vulnerabilities. Their attitudes, personalities, experiences, employment patterns, economic and social pressures all affect them. Some will only become involved in nursery/school life if they are offered sensitive support and understanding. Many will welcome involvement while others may prefer to make minimal contact. There are parents who identify strongly with their ethnic group, religion and cultural practices and others who do not. Assuming that all parents who belong to a particular ethnic, religious or cultural group adopt the customs and traditions of that group, can offend or annoy parents, who may then distance themselves from the nursery/school. Most parents feel that they have the right to say how they would like us to treat their children but not all have the confidence to do so, particularly if we have a very confident professional approach which they find threatening.

Some White parents may feel that their children's education and welfare suffers if there are too many Black children in their nursery/school or if their children are taught other languages and eat 'foreign' foods. At their interview all parents should be told that the nursery/school is run along anti-discriminatory lines and be given a copy of its equality policy.

The active involvement of parents with physical disabilities depends on factors such as physical access into and around the building and appropriate toilet facilities. They might never have been inside a mainstream nursery/school and feel apprehensive and self-conscious. Inaccessible buildings prevent disabled parents from becoming parent governors – who now have significant influence in the running of nurseries/schools. Parents may be worried about reactions to their disability or to their children's.

As the traditional family is still considered to be the norm, single parents often face prejudice, stigmatisation and marginalisation as well as poverty. Fathers who are bringing up their children on their own may be regarded by staff as oddities. It will be hard for them to take part in the life of the nursery/school if gaining acceptance and trust is a problem. Many gay men and lesbian mothers have had children while in heterosexual relationships, others while in homosexual relationships. They are more likely to become involved in the nursery/school if they feel that they are accepted and valued by us and other parents and if they know that we will support their children if they encounter any physical or verbal abuse.

Refugee parents come from many countries and from various national, ethnic, cultural and linguistic backgrounds. They bring with them wide-ranging experiences, qualifications and expertise but many are women who have to cope with their children without the support of their extended families. They may not be fluent in English or have employment skills they need and may feel lonely and depressed.

Some Traveller families live in houses but most live in trailers. There are few sites provided for them so they face constant harassment and pressure to 'move on'. It is the mothers who are mainly responsible for the care of their young children but it is often difficult for them to become involved in nurseries/schools. They may fear hostility from staff and other parents and the sites may be too far away for them to participate. Traditionally in Traveller families girls are expected to take on child-care responsibilities and help their mothers with household chores while boys work with their fathers. Attitudes towards gender roles are embedded in Traveller culture – as they are in many cultures – and may mean that these parents do not agree with all aspects of our anti-discriminatory practice.

Many parents whose own education was based on very different teaching methods, codes of discipline and classroom management have little understanding of the value of play and may think that the discipline in their children's nursery/school is too lax or the teaching too informal. Yeatman (1988) found that some minority ethnic groups had little understanding of the difference between pre-school education and formal schooling. They did not expect their children to play and did not realise that they were learning. A mismatch can develop between the expectations of parents and teachers – as happened to Sho in a school in North London:

> Sho's education in an Infant school and a Japanese Saturday school began at the same time. At first he played for long periods of time with the wide range of play materials on offer in his reception class. With the other children he eagerly pretended to read and write and proudly took his writing home to show his parents. But by the end of the second week Sho seemed to lose interest in playing and he strongly resisted the teacher's efforts to engage him in these activities. She let him be. When he became disruptive, the teacher decided that it was time to have a word with his parents. It quickly became apparent that they had high

aspirations for him and that they were disappointed with his lack of progress. They referred to his efforts at writing as 'rubbish' and compared them unfavourably with his achievements at his Saturday school. They had regarded the teacher as the 'expert' and might have respected what she was doing if she had only taken the time to explain her approach and to find out how Sho was being taught and how he was progressing in his community school.

Parents who can't communicate in English may feel marginalised and isolated and feel that they have little to contribute. As discussed in chapter four, having English as an additional language is too often seen as a problem and parents may be treated accordingly.

Although the perception persists that Black parents are not interested in their children's progress, there is no research evidence to support this view. Black parents are just as concerned as White parents about their children's academic achievements and their all-round development. This is evident in the growth of Black parent groups and the parents' involvement in setting up and running Supplementary/Saturday schools where children are taught by members of the community and do not have to contend with racism.

Racism creates strains and tensions which makes the difficult task of bringing up a family even more difficult. Many parents feel that they have to teach their young children about the realities of racism and, at the same time, encourage them to be whatever they want to be. As the main priority for many Black parents is to provide for their children, building collaborative relationships with staff is unlikely to feature very prominently on their list of priorities. In nurseries/schools that reflect their cultures, parents are more likely to want to be involved. However, if their languages, cultural or religious values are not acknowledged or respected they may feel anxious about the well-being of their children in that environment. Black parents feel very strongly that the racism that their children and they themselves have to face is generally ignored.

In 1994 the Early Years Trainers Anti-Racist Network sent out a questionnaire to parents who were bringing up children in mixed parentage families. They are voices that are not very often heard. These are three of the responses:

I used to think, like most other people who have nothing to do with black people, that skin colour didn't matter – inside we are all the same. Now I know that this is not so. It matters a lot. When you have a black baby, people don't look into the pram to see how lovely your baby is. They look to see what colour the baby is, how dark, what kind of hair the baby has. Sometimes it gets on your nerves. They refer to the child as 'one of them'.

My daughter is six years old and for the last two years she has been consciously tackling racism. I cannot express how sick this makes me feel, that children so young have to struggle, they have to grow up quick and be twice as good as the white child next to them. In shops, assistants look around to find her mother and other children (strangers) ask, 'How come she's brown and you're white?' I feel that I must make every attempt to make this world a better place for my daughter. A tall order but if I don't start then who will?

If only teachers, playgroup personnel and nursery nurses were sufficiently professional and informed to meet us (parents) half way, our task would be easier. ... I am also sickened by the amount of effort our children have to make to fight racism. ... How dare staff leave children as young as four to cope with racism alone? Why is their training so inadequate that they fail to realise the seriousness of the situation and don't have a clue as to how to deal with it?

If Black parents pick up overt or hidden messages from White staff or other parents that they do not belong they may keep their distance.

## Strategies for developing collaborative relationships

Appreciating and understanding one another and having a culturally appropriate curriculum helps us overcome some of the personal and social barriers that limit collaboration. Empathy, understanding and willingness to try new ways of doing things characterise an anti-discriminatory approach to the building of collaborative parent relationships. Where collaboration is successful all parents feel that they 'belong' and are encouraged to identify ways in which they might become further involved. They receive the message that as there is no single 'best' way to bring up children, a range of child rearing practices, including theirs, are valued and respected. The following scenarios described by Brendah Gaine and Anke van Keulen (1997:19) highlight ways in which staff might respond to parents and some possible outcomes:

## Scenario one:
Six month old Rosy cries when she wakes up from her nap. Her care giver, Joanne has begun dressing Mark. She lets Rosy cry while she finishes dressing him (takes about five minutes) and then picks her up. Mrs H, Rosy's mother who has come early to collect Rosy, sees the incident. She attends to Rosy and takes her home. Two days go by. Joanne phones to find out what why Rosy has not been at the Centre. Mrs H says that she'll bring Rosy the next day but she doesn't. She finally comes in on the following Monday. Joanne takes Mrs H aside and asks why Rosy was away. Mrs H says that Rosy was upset and that Joanne didn't take good care of her.

## Response A
Joanne is surprised and hurt.

Joannne:   I take good care of all my babies and would never do any thing to hurt Rosy.

Mrs H:   You let Rosy cry too much.

Joanne:   I was dressing Mark and only let Rosy cry for a few minutes.

Mrs H:   That's not good. In my country we always pick up the baby right away.

Joanne:   In this country we do not believe in spoiling babies and it's good for Rosy to learn that an adult won't come immediately when she cries.

Mrs H looks upset but says nothing more. Joanne decides she has to ensure that Rosy does not become too spoiled so lets her cry a little longer before she attends to her. Rosy cries more often when her mother leaves her in the morning and as she is not thriving, Joanne decides to speak to Mrs H again to find out what is going wrong at home.

## Do you agree?

Joanne acted defensively to justify herself. She neither acknowledged the mother's concern nor did she seem to realise that there are other, equally valid, ways to care for babies. By making no effort to adapt her behaviour to Rosy's family's cultural beliefs and practices and assuming that Rosy's failure to thrive was caused by a problem at home, Joanne made things worse for Rosy. She created an even wider gap between what was done at home and her resolve not to spoil her. She didn't use good communication, negotiation or conflict management skills.

## Response B

Joanne realises immediately that this is a serious issue because Mrs H has never criticised the staff before.

Joanne: I care very much for Rosy and I don't want to hurt her in
any way. Please tell me what I did that wasn't good for Rosy.

Mrs H: You let her cry too long.

Joanne: Was that when I was dressing Mark?

Mrs H nods assent.

Joanne: What would you have done?

Mrs H: I would have picked her up right away. In my country they think a mother who lets her baby cry is not good.

Joanne: So when I didn't pick Rosy up right away, it worried you.

Mrs H: Yes, Rosy will be frightened.

Joanne: Is that why you kept her home the past few days?

Mrs H: I wanted her home with me but now I have to go back to work.

Joanne: I know that it is hard for you to leave Rosy here all day, especially if you think I was doing something that would upset her. I didn't know that letting Rosy cry for what seemed to me like only a little while seemed too long for you. Now that I understand how you feel and what you do

|  | with Rosy at home, I will be more careful about picking her up as soon as she cries. Will that make you feel better about leaving her here? |
|---|---|
| Mrs H smiles: | Yes |
| Joanne: | Rosy may sometimes have to wait a little while to be picked up if another baby needs attention or is in physical danger or is hurt, and if I am the only adult available. Will you feel comfortable with that? |
| Mrs H: | I know there are other babies. I just want to know that Rosy will be safe. |
| Joanne: | I'm glad you let me know why you were unhappy. Please be sure to let me know if anything else I do bothers you. |
| Mrs H: | You tell me also if there is something I need to know. |

After this conversation Joanne realises she had not thought much about how parents handle children's crying. She also wonders if other mothers from the same ethnic background as Mrs H feel the same as Mrs H does. She decides to ask each family.

## Do you agree?

Joanne immediately made it clear that she was open to hearing what had upset Mrs H and responded to her feelings. Joanne accepted that she makes mistakes and showed her willingness to learn so that she could do better. She asked questions to help her get the information she needed to understand why Mrs H was upset and she sought information from the rest of the parents. She was willing to modify her behaviour for Rosy's sake (so she would feel secure), for Mrs H's sake (so she would feel secure about leaving Rosy) and for her own sake (so she could continue a trusting relationship with Mrs H). Mrs H also had to do a little adapting. She had to accept that there could be times when Rosy might have to be left to cry for a little while.

## Scenario two:

Some of the families in a family centre come from an ethnic group who protect their babies against illnesses and other dangers by putting a protective amulet around their neck. But the Centre has a safety regulation which does not allow infants and toddlers to wear necklaces – injuries may be caused by chewing or choking or by other babies pulling them too tight or yanking them off. Or the amulets might be lost. The staff are trying to decide what to do. Some of the suggestions are culturally repressive and others are culturally responsive.

Rosa:     We have a problem. I asked Mrs M about the amulet and she said she never takes it off. The baby could come to harm if she did.

Beth:     What superstition! I don't think we should give in to it. It's very simple – wearing a necklace is against the regulations. Besides, we know that taking off the amulet won't hurt them.

Mark:     We may not think it will but if the families think so, they will be very unhappy and anxious if we remove them

Lynn:     Well, I don't see what else we can do. I feel sympathy for the families but we can't let the kids wear them – it's too dangerous.

Rosa:     It could be but I don't think we can just ask the families to take them off.

Beth:     We're making a big deal out of nothing. Families have to accept the rules and I don't think we should encourage such practices. They're living in this country now.

Rosa:     They're not your religious beliefs but they *are* theirs. They are as important to them as yours are to you.

Lynn:     Let's just tell them we are sorry, but it's not safe and it's against the rules. We can say their children can wear amulets at home and assure them that we have other ways
to        keep the babies safe and well here.

Mark: We need to do more. We have to think about the children's safety from our point of view and theirs and to find solutions that meet the regulations and the families' needs.

Rosa: I can think of one and I'm sure we can think of others. I suggest we ask the parents to take off the amulets when they come in and put them in a special box that we will keep on a shelf in the room. When the children go home, they can put them back on.

Mark: I think we need to ask the families if that will be enough. What if we suggest pinning the amulet to the underside of a child's shirt so that it cannot be pulled?

Lynn: That would be going against the rules.

Mark: We sometimes have to modify a regulation. If the parents don't feel that their children are safe, we won't be able to build a trusting relationship with them even if we know that our regulation is for the children's safety.

Beth: I will not agree to a solution that goes against the regulations.

Rosa: I think we first need to talk with the families before making a decision. They may have other ideas that meet the intention of the regulation.

Mark: When we raise the issue with parents I suggest we explain our safety concerns, what the injuries might be and that accidents can happen quickly even when adults are around. We should ask about the importance of the amulets and assure the parents that we empathise with their viewpoint. Then, together, we can work out a solution acceptable to them and to us.

Rosa and Mark volunteer to meet with the families and report back to the rest of the staff.

## Do you agree?

Beth refused to acknowledge that there was a problem and did not consider asking the parents about their beliefs; her only solution was to remove the amulets. Lynn showed more feeling for the families than Beth and acknowledged that there was a problem but was not interested in learning about the parents' beliefs or willing to make any changes to meet their needs. She saw the safety of the children only from the Centre's perspective. Mark and Rosa knew how to acknowledge, ask about and adapt in order to resolve a problem. They respected the parents and wanted to communicate and work with them. Mark was more willing than Rosa to modify the regulations.

Working collaboratively with parents was the central feature of a six month programme reported by Jacqueline Smikle, Clare Moynihan and Liz-anne des Vignes (1997). Developed to encourage children to learn about, value and respect each other's culture, it drew on the knowledge and interests of the children and their parents and addressed the six key learning areas and desired outcomes inspected by Ofsted.

> The first thing that staff did was to inform the parents by letter about the project and what they hoped to achieve. Parents were asked to give their country of origin and to say which festivals they felt were important in their culture. A second letter was sent two weeks later giving more details and asking parents for their help. Key workers spoke personally to parents, encouraged them to ask questions, explained what help was needed and invited their support. Timetables of activities were displayed so that parents could see what was being done and how they could be involved. Parents were encouraged to join in the activities and go on the outings. They brought artefacts from their homes, talked to the staff about them and sometimes corrected the way they were displayed. They told stories to the children, taught songs in their home languages and ran cooking activities making traditional foods. They told the staff about their festivals, their purpose and how and when they celebrated them. Parents talked to their children about their own backgrounds and traditions and heard about what the children were learning about their own and each other's cultures.

At the end of the project the staff wrote to thank the parents for taking part and asked for their views on how they felt the programme had gone. Here are couple of responses:

> The cultural programme was so valuable because, in order for children to develop, they have to learn about their own culture and also other people's cultures. In that way they will grow up to be better adults and more interesting people.

> The programme was very important for me and my children because I wanted to let them know where I come from and who we are.

The staff team felt that they had learnt to know their own cultures better, to respect other people's cultures and to realise how important they are to them. They developed their skills in working co-operatively with parents and others in the community and appreciated the real benefits of working together – they gained the parents' respect.

## Some practical strategies

The following suggestions are offered as a guide. They can be adapted and extended to suit particular circumstances and conditions.

- Time has to be built into our programme to listen and to respond with interest to parents – even though financial cutbacks, reduction of staff and increased stress and strain make adequate time difficult to find.

- We need to understand the nature of cross-cultural differences and how these can sometimes lead to breakdown in communication. Even differences in accent and intonation can cause misunderstandings.

- Parents with disabilities need to be especially welcomed and helped to feel comfortable. Give a sight impaired parent an initial friendly touch on the arm and a word of introduction, particularly if she/he has not visited before so can't recognise voices. If possible, communicate in sign language with hearing impaired parents, and look directly at anyone who has partial hearing loss.

To ensure that parents in wheelchairs do not feel that they are being talked down to, try to keep at eye level with them and encourage children to do the same. Parents of children with disabilities or debilitating conditions like Sickle Cell Anaemia, Thalassaemia and Tay-Sachs Disease may need support and opportunities to express their anxieties and feelings.

• The initial interview needs to be carefully planned because it can influence future relationships with parents. We need to consider whether an interpreter would be helpful for parents who are not confident about speaking English and to check whether our questions are clear and culturally appropriate. For example, do we ask for a Jewish or Muslim child's Christian name?

• Interviews provide an opportunity for the exchange of information so parents must have the time to ask questions and have them answered to their satisfaction. Refugee families may need special consideration. They may have undergone endless formal interviews with British officials and found them distressing. They may have painful memories of interrogation in their own countries. Spafford and Bolloten (1995) suggest that these families must be made especially welcome as they are probably trying to deal with disruption, poverty, uncertainty and, if they are Black, racism as well.

• All parents need to know that the nursery/school follows an anti-discriminatory approach and they should be given a copy of our equality policy. Parents need to understand that the service operates on the principles enshrined in the policy and appreciate what this means regarding their children's learning and behaviour. Before introducing programmes to promote collaboration, we need to discuss the aims with parents and decide together how these could best be achieved.

• As many parents as possible should be involved when developing, implementing and monitoring the equality policy. The principles on which the policy is to be based have to be worked out – these principles are not negotiable. The detail of whom the policy should cover and how it should operate needs to be agreed and constantly reviewed.

- Parents need to be consulted to ensure that the resources reflect the diversity of cultures and lifestyles represented in the nursery/ school. Invite parents from minority and majority ethnic groups to bring in pictures of members of their family, celebrations and rituals, outings and holidays. When outings are planned, the transport provided and the destination must be accessible for any parents or children who are physically disabled. Wherever possible notices in the nursery/school and those that are sent home should be translated into the home languages of the children. Take care that discussions and written communications do not transmit the message that 'professionals know best'. Avoid using jargon or patronising language, and provide information on parenting and where parents can get support.

- Talk to parents about the activities being offered and why they are offered so that they can understand their value. Invite them to make suggestions. Parents who have come from areas where water is scarce and precious may be upset by the way children are encouraged to play with it and 'waste' it. Others may be worried that their children will become ill if they play with sand – as happened in a daycare centre in Deptford:

  > I was showing a Vietnamese parent around the centre, explaining the program. When we arrived at the sand-pit the parent looked very uncertain. My Vietnamese-speaking bilingual worker explained the value of sand play and after some discussion we discovered that in Vietnam the sand came from a particularly polluted river. Discussion with another bilingual worker revealed that a family from El-Salvador had expressed similar concerns. The parents were reassured when we explained that the sand was bought especially for the children to play with and was perfectly safe.

- Promote parental involvement by being flexible about times for meetings and social events, ensuring that venues are accessible, reflecting cultural diversity and providing créches or paying babysitting fees. By celebrating festivals together, parents share their knowledge and come together socially. Such an occasion is often the first time that Black and White, abled and disabled parents meet each other in a social setting. It may be possible to respond to parents by, for example, having birthday and other celebrations at the end of the day thus allowing Jehovah's Witness parents the option to pick their children up early although this could be a problem if parents are working.

• Building on parents interests and their ability to support one another, can lead to setting up groups or attending classes together. At the Centre where she is the Head, Margy Whalley (1994:113) describes how some of their parent groups developed:

'Groups with a 'child-centred' orientation evolved into groups which dealt with adult issues and focused on parents' needs. ... A series of groups was set up which was concerned with supporting parents; these identified 'life issues' including bringing up children and the single parent or having a child with special needs. ... Open University study groups have been an important part of our community-education package.'

• Deal with conflicts carefully and sensitively and strive for solutions that are acceptable to staff and to the parents. Changing deeply embedded beliefs, values and attitudes which are bound up with a person's sense of self generally provokes inner conflict, insecurity and confusion. Conflicts between staff and parents are likely to be difficult to resolve if the views of both involve strongly held beliefs. The goal is for both parties to express their feelings in a respectful way, listen to each other's point of view and negotiate a resolution of the conflict that both can accept. If either party feels threatened, they may react aggressively, refuse to consider alternatives and the encounter could produce a hardening of attitudes instead of generating change. Staff discussions and inservice anti-discriminatory training can help to ensure that fairness and equity are preserved while cultural norms and values are respected. We may feel ill-equipped or too stressed to handle this responsibility. However, as the next chapter shows, on-going inservice anti-discriminatory training can offer support, develop confidence and the ability to listen and communicate effectively with parents. And training in conflict management can help us cope with conflict in a constructive way.

The aim when working collaboratively is to inform and empower parents rather than advise and guide them. They need encouragement and the opportunity to share ideas with people who may be more skilled but are also sufficiently empathetic to be able to offer support.

Many early years educators have drawn inspiration from the philosophy being put into practice in the pre-schools in Reggio Emilia in Italy where, according to Wendy Scott (1997:1):

> The parental role and the efforts of people working with young children are valued and children's own ideas are respected. It is inspiring for us in Britain to see what can be done when parents, professionals and politicians co-operate in giving expression to a strong belief in the importance of early education.

Gilkes (1987) offers us all a vision for the future:

> It [the nursery centre] should reduce conflict between parents and professionals and create community cooperation to maximise our common resources for the benefit of the young child and the family. .... What we want is parent, professional, volunteer, administrator, academic and trainer working cooperatively towards a unified pre-school service which is flexible, free and a wonderful place to work regardless of age, colour or gender.

# Chapter 7
# Not too Old to Learn

*Not everything that is faced can be changed, but nothing can be changed until it is faced.* James Baldwin

This chapter looks at inservice training. On-going anti-discriminatory training builds on existing knowledge and skills and gives educators the confidence and support they need to work effectively according to anti-discriminatory principles. Training clarifies the processes that White people go through as they come to acknowledge and understand White privilege and the processes Black people go through in the course of uncovering and coming to terms with internalised oppression. Challenging sexism, class, homophobia and ablism are all considered, along with positive ways of dealing with conflict.

'Learning is a life-long process' may be a cliché but it certainly applies to everybody working within an anti-discriminatory framework. We are all travelling along a road that has no end – educators who have been striving for years to combat discrimination, those who have recently begun and those who oppose discrimination in principle but need to acquire the relevant knowledge and skills. Others have learned to give the right and expected response without understanding or believing in what they are saying. Attending an occasional conference on equality issues or participating on a one-off training course can be helpful but it is usually not enough to provide commitment or the confidence to reshape practice. Myers (1985:30) describes a typical situation where only lip-service is paid to challenging discrimination and underlines the need for on-going staff development:

> A nursery teacher reported how she changed the Wendy House to the Home Corner and painstakingly encouraged the boys to use this area of the classroom. She was subsequently horrified to hear a classroom assistant tell two boys who were playing with the dressing up clothes that boys didn't do that sort of thing and wouldn't they prefer to play with the lego.

Incidents like this provide informal training opportunities. Gently unpacking comments like this one and helping the person who said it to appreciate its implications, can help her/him to understand the issues. But it requires discretion and very sensitive handling to prevent a defensive reaction – generally an attempt to trivialise the comment and block the entire issue.

## Training for change

Training is designed to achieve a heightened awareness of issues and to develop deeper understanding, empathy and trust. Participants can use the space, time and opportunities that training provides to extend their existing knowledge and skills and keep informed of current thinking by:

* developing their awareness and understanding of how social inequalities affect the life chances of the families with whom they work

* examining their own misconceptions and fears, talking about their own stereotypical views and considering how these became internalised and the purpose they served

* enhancing their awareness of how power operates in society and in their nursery/school and suggesting strategies to bring about change. By gaining greater insight into their own and other people's feelings, especially when they are in unequal relationships, can help educators understand how parents and children might feel

* increasing their understanding of internalised oppression and internalised privilege and examining how they as individuals may be

participating in their own oppression and the oppression of others. For example, in their enthusiasm to change sexist attitudes and practices they may have unconsciously adopted a racist and culturally oppressive approach

• deepening their understanding of why it is important to do antidiscriminatory work in all-White settings too, and to explore and validate the diverse cultures often concealed within White groups

• learning about their own cultural background and about cultures other than their own, how to adapt their teaching style and curriculum content accordingly, and how to work with others to change individual and institutional discriminatory practices

• deepening understanding of what cultures can mean to people. For example, appreciating the group power and strength that culture provides, heightening awareness and appreciation of the values and beliefs that underlie practices such as child rearing and ensuring that the provision that children are offered fits comfortably with their home experiences

• feeling comfortable with themselves and feeling that their contribution in the workplace makes a difference

• developing their motivation to identify and counter discriminatory structures, attitudes and practices and to create an environment in which all children and their families feel equally valued and respected

• acquiring more knowledge about relevant legislation such as the Race Relations Act (1976) and the Children Act (1989), so that they can use them appropriately

• recognising that children are growing up in a world in which cross-cultural contact is a fact of life both within and across national borders. Children are culturally enriched when they know about the cultures of people who are different from themselves, are keen to learn more about them and can speak languages additional to their home language(s).

Although shortage of funds seriously restricts the possibilities for educators to be able to maintain on-going anti-discriminatory training it is an ideal which is worth striving for. If only the working conditions in the pre-schools in Emilia Romagna could be implemented in all British nurseries/schools, educators would have the time and the right to extend themselves professionally and personally. Mary Jane Drummond (1997:29) describes how the educators she met on her visit to Italy are given time to think, reflect and to talk to colleagues and parents:

> In nursery schools in Emilia Romagna, the educators work a thirty six hour week, of which six hours a week, every week, is non-contact time. Some of this is designated for administration and practical organisation but the rest is dedicated to professional development: work on curriculum and pedagogy, work with parents, work with their co-ordinators. These educators have four or five hours a week to spend together, thinking and learning.

## Focusing on change

Most anti-discriminatory training programmes provide information about the historical, political, social and economic conditions which create inequality and oppression. The more we understand the forces that are influencing our lives and those of our colleagues, the more likely we are to improve our professional practice. Always remember that although oppressions are deeply rooted and inter-linked they were instituted, developed and perpetuated by people, so they can be eliminated by people.

As educators we know that Black people, Travellers, refugees, women, working class people and lesbians and gays all experience oppression. However, some of us may not have understood what they face, or realised that what they experience, how they experience it, and the degree to which they experience it varies between and within groups. These are just a few:

• Although Black women and White are linked in their oppression they are separated by ethnicity. On the power ladder, White women may be two steps removed from power but Black women are three steps removed.

- A large number of people with disabilities are living in poverty because they cannot find work, and social security benefits are inadequate. Black people with disabilities are accorded lower status than disabled White people and racism reduces their opportunities in the crucial areas of employment, housing and education.

- White and Black men and women who are unemployed and poorly paid experience poverty, discrimination and powerlessness. They are all in the same boat, but racism puts them on different decks.

- A growing number of talented, confident Black women and men are working in a range of professions such as medicine, law, education, caring, accountancy and the arts but their success is seldom acknowledged – they tend to be invisible. Their life-styles are likely to have more in common with their White middle class neighbours than with Black people living in poor housing in the inner cities – although they are likely to experience racism whatever their class position.

As educators most of us would like to counter discrimination but we do not know enough about the historical background or how social inequalities operate in Britain today and how we ourselves may be contributing to their perpetuation. We may be unaware that groups and individuals who are oppressed act as oppressors of other groups and individuals, usually unconsciously, but nevertheless with far-reaching consequences. The many different groupings and voices within the feminist movement provide one example:

Some White feminists loudly condemn racism but the majority have alienated Black women because they have not confronted racism and cultural oppression within their ranks. Black women strongly assert their right to seek their own liberation without being patronised by women who think they can do it for them. Moreover, the feminist movement has been dominated by middle class women who have contributed to working class women's disempowerment by not listening to or addressing their concerns over issues such as pay and job discrimination. Many feminists believe that the liberation of women necessitates the liberation of all human beings. Doesn't this entail the women's movement being committed to fighting racism and addressing issues that are of concern to Black and White working class women?

Both Irish people and Jewish people have a long history of oppression but they benefit from White privilege and can merge with other Whites – an option not open to Black people. Although many in the Irish and the Jewish communities are involved in challenging racism, many more participate, consciously or unconsciously, in perpetuating individual and institutional practices which discriminate against Black people. Being Irish or Jewish does not insulate educators from the influence of prevailing racist attitudes and practices.

Many White people do not realise that their white skin puts them in a privileged position. Mathias and French (1996:xxi) quote the words of one woman on recognising the implications of being White:

> As a White person, I was taught to see racism only in individual acts of meanness, not in invisible systems conferring dominance on my racial group. I think Whites are carefully taught not to recognise White privilege, as males are taught not to recognise male privilege. I have come to see White privilege as an invisible package of unearned assets which I can count on cashing in each day ... Whites are taught to think of their lives as morally neutral, normative, average and also ideal, so that when we work to benefit others, this is seen as work which will allow them to be more like 'us'.

White educators from working class backgrounds may not believe that they benefit from being White, that they experience White privilege. 'Don't tell me I'm privileged! I grew up poor and I'm still struggling', they often say. Their sense of being powerless outsiders prevents them from seeing themselves as part of the White power structure. Power is not primarily a personal issue but is based on a hierarchically structured system designed to get maximum benefit from maximum division – divide and rule. So when members of White oppressed groups fail to understand the parallels between their experience and those of Black people, they are allowing a wedge to be driven between them clouding their understanding of the issues and restricting their ability to bring about meaningful change. Although all White people do not consciously or equally profit from racism and a number are actively involved in transforming the system, having a White skin still privileges them. Although Black people can be personally prejudiced towards White people they do not have the institutional power to oppress them.

Racism is such a sensitive subject that it is not surprising that talking about it evokes so much emotion. Outpourings of negative feelings can destroy the trust and empathy on which successful training depends but the damage can be limited if trainers are aware of how the processes of uncovering internalised oppression and White privilege are affecting the participants and can anticipate where conflicts are likely to arise and use conflict management strategies to deal with them. Such skills are useful when working with children and parents and relating to people outside the nursery/school. Participants may become more sensitively aware of how a Black person might feel in an all-White setting. Annan (1993:100) describes his experience:

> ... as a black teacher I am continually made conscious that most primary schools are predominately white, and for that matter, middle class, institutions. ... (I was once challenged by a school-keeper as soon as I entered the playground – even by being there I apparently constituted a threat). In staff rooms, there are generally two opposite tendencies, one of which is to ignore the fact of dif-ference, while the other is to continually highlight it, by referring all equal opportunities to the black teacher. ... The issues involved in being a black male primary teacher are complex, due to racial bias found both in schools and in society as a whole, but I believe they are worthy of some serious thought and debate.

The focus of the training programme is on challenging racism but many of the strategies employed and the stages that participants go through apply when challenging other social inequalities.

## White privilege/internalised oppression: two sides of one coin

Louise Derman-Sparks (1993) suggests that everybody goes through a series of stages. These are different for White people with their ex-perience of privilege and for Black people with their experience of oppression. This is how she describes them:

## Stage one: *Denial/Resistance*

During this stage White people make statements like: things are much better these days so why reopen the issue; slavery happened a long time ago before we were born so it has nothing to do with us; we're not prejudiced and we don't notice if people are black, brown, green or purple (the colour-blind approach – this ridiculing of skin colour is always directed to the 'other').

For White people the stage is characterised by:

• lack of awareness

• lack of knowledge

• denial – deep-sleep

• a colour-blind approach

• individualism

• no sense of personal responsibility

• defensiveness

For Black people the stage is characterised by:

• assimilation/cultural alienation

• denial (I don't experience racism)

• defensiveness (don't rock the boat)

• hopelessness.

## Stage two: *Disequilibrium*

For White people this is a difficult phase and it can be hard for the trainers too as they may be the target for blame. The objective is to help people uncover their feelings and talk about them and to get them to recognise that other people are having similar feelings – that it is a shared experience. Once people have reached this point they need to move on to look at how they as Whites want to act, how they are going to learn about their own culture and how they are going to act in antiracist ways.

So in this stage White people are:

- beginning to face realities of institutional racism

- beginning to face realities of their own participation and being absorbed by feeling pain, sorrow, guilt, shame, anger and letting these emotions rule them

- projecting blame

- re-examining White identity and not liking being White

- demanding that Black people tell them what to do; not yet taking responsibility for change.

For Black people this is also a difficult and highly emotional stage. They may find it too painful and not want the coping strategies they have developed to be disturbed. This is a protective mechanism, not wanting to reopen the wound but it is important for them to look at how they have learnt to deal with racism and what kind of identity they have created in the process. They may recognise that they have colluded with racism, that they have subscribed to some of the beliefs, the negative messages about their group, so that deep down they believe some of them – they have internalised their oppression. Anger they have felt but swallowed and suppressed comes flooding out – a bit like a pressure cooker letting off steam. The trainers have to be prepared to help people at this stage to express these feelings but also to move them on to think about what they want to learn about their own identity, history and culture and what they are going to do with their anger. Having thought about and talked about these questions usually enables people to move on.

Black people in this stage are:

- re-awakening/sharpening conflicts caused by racism

- opening up old wounds

- letting emotions of anger and rage take over

- becoming aware of internalised oppression

- re-examining group identity

- immersing themselves in their own group

- re-examining their role as activists

- feeling frustrated with Whites and with the slow pace of change.

## Stage three: *Reconstruction*
For White people this stage is characterised by:

- working to understand the nature, dynamics and history of racism

- beginning to accept the realities of institutional racism and of White privilege

- constructing a different view of society

- developing an understanding about how racism impacts on their own and others' social and psychological development

- recognising themselves as cultural beings

- becoming activists: channelling pain/anger/guilt into productive work and taking responsibility for personal, professional and institutional change

- creating 'new White' identities as antiracists and accepting their connection to other Whites

- building equitable, self-reflective relationships with Black people

For Black people this stage is characterised by:

- building an understanding of the nature, dynamics and history of racism

- building their understanding about the impact of racism on people's social and psychological development

- reclaiming or re-integrating their group identity

- increasing their knowledge about their group's history and culture

- becoming activists and thus channelling pain/anger/frustration into productive work to bring about personal, professional and institutional change

• building relationships and coalitions with other Black people

• building relationships and coalitions with White people

• functioning biculturally.

Derman-Sparks points out that if trainers find themselves with Whites in denial and Blacks who are saying that they don't want to talk about the issue, everybody gets along very well on the surface but all the upheaval is going on under cover. If Black people have reached the stage of reconstruction of antiracist work and White people have also reached this stage, there can be real in-depth dialogue and they can begin working together. However, difficulties will almost inevitably arise with all the other combinations of stages, the hardest being when people are in stage two. Whites are feeling guilty, ashamed, projecting blame on others, and Blacks are furious about racism. An unhealthy dynamic can develop where Black people have a captive audience with whom to be angry and which will in turn feed the White people's guilt. In this situation nothing gets done; nobody changes their ideas or their practice.

To complicate matters further, trainers also go through these developmental stages. Sometimes they are in the disequilibrium stage so White trainers working with Whites will want to make everyone else feel guilty just as they do. It is obviously not right that trainers work out their developmental stages on the people they are training. A support group can enable them to work on issues together.

## Conflict management
Both conflict management and anti-discriminatory training call for open communication, a valuing of diversity, respect and trust, and the development of empathy and understanding. They both require participants to be willing to listen to and consider new ideas, to explore feelings, reflect and act. Conflict management is particularly effective when one of the objectives of the inservice anti-discriminatory training programme is team building. Using this approach the trainer can act as a role model and provide activities and tasks that involve planning and working towards common goals, helping to change perceptions in the process. People tend to view conflict in negative terms – their own

experiences have perhaps involved aggressive and confrontational behaviour and bullying. Resolution of conflict can ultimately enrich a relationship and be liberating.

Conflict management requires us to:

* understand the causes of conflict

* recognise, name and express feelings appropriately

* handle anger effectively

* develop a broad range of communication skills including active listening and reframing

* step into other people's shoes.

We have noted how change and conflict frequently go hand in hand, especially where people feel that their way of thinking and acting are under threat. This is because changing deeply embedded beliefs, values and attitudes which are bound up with people's sense of self generally creates inner conflict, insecurity and confusion. Consequently, conflict between colleagues or between educators and parents is likely to be difficult to resolve if the views of both involve their strongly held beliefs. Conflict will probably escalate if the parties blame and judge, take up rigid positions, jump to conclusions, or if emotion takes over. But if the parties acknowledge each other's feelings and needs, and if they seek common ground, co-operate and aim for a win-win resolution then conflict can de-escalate.

In conflict situations people commonly blame one another – but this is not helpful. Being trapped in cycles of mutual blame keeps people locked in the past and does not encourage healing and growth. A more helpful approach is for them to see the conflict as a mutual problem to be solved together rather than as a battle to be won. The goal is for both parties to express their feelings in a respectful way, listen to each other's point of view and negotiate a resolution of the conflict. Encouraging collaborative creative thinking often results in co-operative rather than competitive solutions. Simulation games, drama and role-plays will give participants opportunities to practice their conflict resolution skills and can be particularly useful in scenarios where conflict is played out between people from groups that face discrimination and those that don't. It can be a painful and illuminating learning experience for those participants who unwittingly adopt an oppressive approach. As Mary Jane Drummond (1993) says: .... *there's got to be personal learning – which is emotional, untidy, risky, sometimes unpleasant. Looking into the mirror is not always a rewarding experience.*

## Using the law

Information about legislation and suggestions on how it can be used are generally included in anti-discriminatory training programmes. Everyone involved with the care and education of young children needs to know how the law may be affecting their practice – whether, in fact, they are complying with the law. Knowledge of the law can also be used to persuade people to change their direct or indirect discriminatory practice. This is especially important for registration and inspection officers. Jane Lane (1996:77), for many years Education Officer at the Commission for Racial Equality argues that:

> The Race Relations Act requires equal treatment to be given to people of all racial groups so long as the action referred to is covered by sections of the Act i.e. it is unlawful to discriminate on racial grounds. The Children Act, unlike other Acts, does not say what you must *not* do – it says what you *must* do.

The most relevant laws, at the time of writing this book, are the Sex Discrimination Act (1975), the Race Relations Act (1976), the Education Reform Act (1988), the Children Act (1989) and the Disability Discrimination Act (1995). Any new anti-discriminatory legislation or any legislation that has equality implications should be included in future anti-discriminatory training programmes. This could help educators who are framing responses to consultation documents from Government Departments to draw attention to any discriminatory features that may have been overlooked.

Once concepts such as direct and indirect discrimination and children in need have been identified and understood, trainers could trigger discussion using examples suggested by Jane Lane:

A multiracial nursery school prides itself on having an antiracist policy and is pleased to have such a culturally diverse range of children. It operates a waiting list of the names of children who wish to attend the school, on a first come first served basis.

The local authority has set up a site for Travellers. The chairperson of a playgroup management committee tells the playgroup that if any 'Romany Gypsy' children apply to attend, they must say that the playgroup does not take 'Romany Gypsy' children because they have caused trouble in the past. Is this lawful? What should the registration officer do, with regard to the Children Act?

A voluntary organisation running a support service for Somali refugee mothers and children advertises for a worker, 'who must be able to speak Somali'. Is this lawful?

An infant school in a largely White area takes students on placement from the local training college. A Black student is sent to them. The officer in charge tells the college that they do not want her there because she won't feel comfortable as all the children and staff are White. Is she in breach of the Race Relations Act?

A childminder refuses to provide halal, kosher, or vegetarian food. Should she be refused registration under the Children Act?

Trainers may suggest that participants refer to booklets published by the Commission for Racial Equality, such as Lane (1996b) to obtain more detailed information and to make sure that they are not breaking the law. To derive maximum benefit from on-going training, educators need to have time and space between training sessions to express their feelings about the training, extend the knowledge, skills and insights they gained, discuss issues that were raised and identify those they would like included in the next programme.

## Nurture the future

Armed with the knowledge, skills and heightened awareness they have gained from their anti-discriminatory training, educators are likely to be highly motivated to achieve the goal as set by Cummins (1996) which is to create in their nursery/school a model of a caring society that they would like the children to inherit.

It is hoped that educators who attend on-going inservice anti-discriminatory training will identify with the response of one postgraduate student after a 15 week Racism and Human Development course run by Louise Derman-Sparks and Carol Brunson-Phillips (1997:137):

> Tonight was our last class. I've been thinking about why it affects people so much. I think it's because, in untying the knot, you're unravelling the web of lies that each of us has inevitably experienced, and racism is only a part of the false information each of us received while growing up. Racism is the part that is the most obvious and blatant. There are many parts that have taken their dehumanising toll, and in unravelling even a bit of the whole, we feel tremendously excited. We have only to unravel more of it to reclaim ourselves more completely.

## A final word

Nobody ever said that struggling against injustice and oppression would be easy. However, as educators we do have a responsibility and the power to effect change. Even if it seems at times that we are going backwards and at others that progress is so slow that we appear to be standing still our input does make a difference. We can draw strength and encouragement from the fact that equality principles are incorporated in British legislation and that ground breaking, influential and inspiring documents like the American Declaration of Independence, the United Nations Convention on the Rights of the Child, and more recently, the new South African Constitution, enshrine the ideals towards which we are working. The struggle continues and we must continue to struggle actively to transform society so that all children can grow up free from racism, sexism and other forms of discrimination. Accepting the Nobel Peace Prize in 1993 President Nelson Mandela said:

> At the southern tip of Africa, a rich reward is in the making ... an invaluable gift for those who suffered in the name of humanity when they sacrificed everything for liberty, peace and human fulfilment. [The reward is] not to be measured in money ... It must be measured by the happiness of children, the most valuable citizens in any society and the greatest of our treasures.

Chapter 8

# Resourcing for Equality

It is heartening to see how the quality, range and availability of toys, books and other learning materials for the early years has expanded and developed. The resource information that follows is offered as a guide and does not claim to be a comprehensive list of all the suppliers and organisations that counter discrimination, promote respect for a range of lifestyles and cultures and provide support and guidance.

### SUPPLIERS OF POSITIVE IMAGES

ACORN PERCUSSION Unit 34, Abbey Business Centre Ingate Place London SW8 Tel: 0171 720 2243 have a wide range of instruments, to suit all age groups and abilities from pre-school to 16 plus, including special needs.

ALEXANDRA GALLERIES 7 Eileen Road London SE25 5EJ Tel: 0181 684 4123 specialises in the sale and distribution of Contemporary African American fine art prints and posters. Their catalogue, features a full colour range of positive images depicting all aspects of black culture.

AMS EDUCATIONAL Woodside Trading Estate, Low Lane Leeds LS18 5NY Tel: 0113 258 0309 distributes a range of multicultural resources including many produced by the ILEA.

ASCO EDUCATIONAL SUPPLIES Asco House 19 Lockwood Way Parkside Leeds LS11 5TH Tel: 0113 2707070 sells a range of resources including a set of attractive puzzles entitled Children of the World.

BANGLADESH RESOURCE and MULTICULTURAL BOOK CENTRE 1st Floor, 23 Hessel Street London E1 2LR Tel: 0171 488 4243 stocks a range of dolls, toys, books, handicrafts, musical instruments and clothing.

BLACK RIVER BOOKS 113 Stokes Croft Bristol BS1 3RW Tel: 0117 942 3804 publish children's books, posters and greeting cards and stock educational and children's books.

CENTRE FOR MULTICULTURAL EDUCATION Harrison Road Leicester LE4 6RB Tel: 0116 266 5451 have a variety of useful learning materials.

COMMUNITY INSIGHT at Pembroke Centre Cheney Manor Swindon SN2 2PQ Tel: 01793 512612 carries books focusing on child development and equality issues for adults while their children's books complement anti-discriminatory practice.

EARLY YEARS TRAINERS ANTI-RACIST NETWORK, EYTARN, PO Box 28 Wallasey L45 9NP Tel: 0151 639 6136 stocks a set of six beautiful full colour A2 posters and postcards of young children and a range of books designed for initial and in-service training programmes.

EASTSIDE BOOKS 178 Whitechapel Road London E1 1BJ Tel: 0171 247 0216 specialises in working with schools and voluntary groups to increase access to books and reading.

EBONY EYES RAG DOLLS 10 Searson House London SE17 3AY Tel: 0171 735 2887 are black 'cabbage-patch' type dolls and hand puppets and supplies African arts and crafts.

EDU-PLAY at Vulcan Business Centre Units H and I Vulcan Road Leicester LE5 3EB Tel: 0116 262 5827 has resources for play/therapy, learning difficulties and early learning.

EQUALITY LEARNING CENTRE 356 Holloway Road London N7 6PA Tel: 0171 700 8127 stocks a comprehensive range of resources including A3 full colour posters featuring Save the Children projects.

FOREST BOOKSHOP 8 St John Street Coleford Gloucestershire GL16 8AR Tel: 01594 833858 specialises in books on deafness and deaf issues. Their mail order catalogue includes several children's books which incorporate sign language and finger spelling.

GALT EDUCATIONAL Brookfield Road Cheadle Cheshire SK8 2PN Tel: 0161 428 8511 distributes an extensive range of play equipment including the Dara doll, sets of callipers, spectacles and hearing aids.

HARINGEY TRAVELLER SUPPORT TEAM at Education Support Service, The Lodge, Church Lane London N17 8BX Tel: 0181 808 7604 has a range of resources.

INVICTA BOOK SERVICE 162 Coppice Street, Oldham OL8 4BJ Tel: 0161 620 63981 specialises in non-racist and non-sexist publications.

KNOCK ON WOOD at Granary Wharf Leeds LS1 4BR Tel: 0113 2429 146 supplies a comprehensive range of music, instruments, books and recordings.

LETTERBOX LIBRARY Unit 2D Leroy House 436 Essex Road London N1 3QP Tel: 0171 226 1633 is the only book club to specialise in non-sexist and multicultural books for children as well as books about children living in non-traditional families, children with disabilities, and refugees. The books are carefully chosen and the catalogue provides accurate descriptions.

MINORITY GROUP SUPPORT SERVICE Southfields South Street Coventry CV1 5EJ Tel: 01203 226 888 stocks a range of useful materials.

MULTICULTURAL BOOKSHOP Rachid House Westgate Bradford BD1 3AA Tel: 0127 473 1908 stocks posters, artifacts and videos from pre-school to graduate level.

MULTICULTURAL EDUCATION RESOURCES COUNTY SERVICE (MERCS) 66 Cedar Road Bedford MK42 0JE Tel: 0123 436 4475 stocks a variety of resources to promote antiracist/multicultural education.

MULTICULTURAL STUDY CENTRE 451 High Road London N12 0AS Tel: 0181 359 3880 provides support and information on all aspects of equality.

NESARNOLD Ludlow Hill Road West Bridgeford Nottingham NG2 6HD Tel: 01159 452201 distributes a wide range of play equipment including Down's Syndrome dolls and a range of accessories for dolls including a wheel chair, hearing aids, crutches, and spectacles.

NEWS FROM NOWHERE at 112 Bold Street Liverpool L1. Tel: 0151 708 7270 is a feminist bookshop.

NOTHING BUT POSTERS 5 Woodcliffe Drive Chislehurst Kent BR7 5NT Tel: 0171 613 0838 offers a set of 12 A4 laminated posters featuring positive images of young children.

PICTORIAL CHARTS EDUCATIONAL TRUST 27 Kirchen Road London W13 0UD. Tel 0181 567 9206 provides informative and attractive charts for religious studies.

PLAYMATTERS (NATIONAL TOY LIBRARIES ASSOCIATION) 68 Church Way London NW1 1LT Tel: 0171 387 9592 stocks books and toys for children with disabilities.

POSITIVE CHOICES 10 Hazelbank Road London SE6 1TL Tel: 0181 695 0072 makes handmade puzzles from personal photographs.

POSITIVE IMAGE 196a Roundhay Road Leeds LS8 5AA Tel: 0113 293-5550 stocks an extensive range of posters, cards and art and crafts.

PRE-SCHOOL EDUCATION RESOURCE CENTRE 2-4 Roscoe Street Liverpool L1 2SX Tel: 0151 708 7698 supplies a range of play materials.

RADDLE BOOKS 70 Berners Street Leicester LE2 0AF Tel: 0116 262 4875 specialises in African, Caribbean and African-American books, arts/crafts and records.

REDI HOBBIES 4 Hawthorne Cottages, Redehall Road, Horley RH6 9RL Tel: 01342 717538 produces colourful wooden puzzles.

ROY YATES BOOKS Smallfields Cottage, Cox Green, Horsham RH12 3DE Tel: 0140 382 2299 specialises in dual-language books for children.

SEED PUBLICATIONS PO Box 852 London W11 4RY Tel: 0171 603 8523 publishes books, greeting cards and posters. Catalogue available.

SOMA BOOKS LTD 38 Kennington Jane Lane London SE11 4LS Tel: 0171 735 2101 carries an extensive stock of books from India for children and adults.

STEP BY STEP is a mail-order company at Lavenham Road Beeches Trading Estate Bristol BS17 5QX Tel: 0145 432 0999 which specialises in products for young children.

TAMARIND LTD. PO Box 296 Camberley Surrey GU15 1QW Tel: 01276 683 979 produces books, puzzles and sequence cards which challenge ethnic and gender stereotyping.

ZUMA ART SERVICES at Unit V2 Lenton Business Centre Lenton Boulevarde Nottingham NG7 2BD Tel: 0115 952 1961 are large importers of posters.

## SUPPORTIVE ORGANISATIONS

ADVISORY COUNCIL FOR THE EDUCATION OF ROMANY AND OTHER TRAVELLERS Moot House The Stow Harlow CM20 3AG Tel: 01279 418666

ANTI-RACIST TEACHER EDUCATION NETWORK (ARTEN) c\o Samida Garg 28 Sandish Edge, London Road, Hemel Hempstead HB3 9SZ.

ASSOCIATION OF BLIND ASIANS 322 Upper Street London N1 2 XQ Tel: 0171 226 1950.

BLACK CHILDCARE NETWORK 17 Brownhill Road London SE6 2EG Tel: 0181 648 9129.

CHILD POVERTY ACTION GROUP 1 Bath Street London EC1V 9PY Tel: 0171 253 3406

CHILDREN IN SCOTLAND 5 Shandwick Place Edinburgh EH2 4RG Tel: 0131 228 8484.

THE CHILDREN'S RIGHTS OFFICE 319 City Road London EC1V 1LJ Tel: 0171 278 8222

COMMISSION FOR RACIAL EQUALITY Elliot House, Allington Street, London SW1E 5EH Tel: 0171 8828 7022.

DAYCARE TRUST Wesley House, Wild Court London WC2B 5AU Tel: 0171 405 5617/8.

DUBLIN TRAVELLERS EDUCATION & DEVELOPMENT GROUP Pavee Point North Great Charles Street Dublin 1 Tel: 01001 732802

EARLY CHILDHOOD UNIT – National Children's Bureau, 8 Wakley Street London EC1V 7QE Tel: 0171 278 9441.

EARLY YEARS TRAINERS ANTI-RACIST NETWORK, EYTARN, PO Box 28, Wallasey L45 9NP Tel: 0151 639 6136.

EDUCATION CENTRE FOR TRAVELLING CHILDREN Sendy Base Bradford BD4 7PS Tel: 01274 370 143

EQUALITY LEARNING CENTRE 356 Holloway Road London N7 6PA. Tel: 0171 700 8127.

EQUAL OPPORTUNITIES COMMISSION Quay Street Manchester Tel: 0161 833 9244.

GINGERBREAD ASSOCIATION FOR ONE PARENT FAMILIES 16 Clerkenwell Close London EC1 Tel: 0181 336 8183

HARINGEY TRAVELLER SUPPORT TEAM at Education Support Service, The Lodge, Church Lane London N17 8BX Tel: 0181 808 7604

INSTITUTE OF RACE RELATIONS 2 Leeke Street London WC1X 9HS Tel: 0171 837 0041

KIDS CLUB NETWORK Bellerive House 3 Muirfield Crescent London E14 9SZ Tel: 0171 512 2112

MINORITY RIGHTS GROUP 29 Craven Street London WC2N 1UL Tel: 0171 930 6659

NATIONAL ASSOCIATION OF TEACHERS OF TRAVELLERS The Graisley Centre, Pool Street Wolverhampton Tel: 01902 714 646

NATIONAL CHILDMINDING ASSOCIATION 8 Masons Hill, Bromley BR2 9EY Tel: 0181 464 6164.

NATIONAL COUNCIL OF VOLUNTARY CHILD CARE ORGANISA-TIONS 80 White Lion Street London N1 9PF Tel 0171 833 3319.

NATIONAL EARLY YEARS NETWORK (formally VOLCUF) 77 Holloway Road London N7 Tel: 0171 607 9573.

ORGANISATION OF BLIND AFRO CARIBBEANS 24 Hayward House Benhill Road London SE5 7NA Tel: 0171 703 3688.

PRE-SCHOOL LEARNING ALLIANCE (PLA) 61 Kings Cross Road London WC1X 9LL Tel: 0171 833 0991.

PLAYTRAIN 31 Farm Road Birmingham B11 1LS Tel: 0121 766 8446.

SAVE THE CHILDREN 17 Grove Lane London SE5 Tel 0171 703 5400.

SICKLE CELL SOCIETY 54 Station Road London NW10 7UA Tel: 0181 961 7795.

WORKING FOR CHILDCARE 77 Holloway Road London N7 8JZ Tel: 0171 700 0281.

WORKING GROUP AGAINST RACISM IN CHILDRENS RESOURCES 460 Wandsworth Road London SW8 3LX Tel: 0171 627 4594.

## SOME RELEVANT VIDEOS

ALTOGETHER BETTER is a pack containing a booklet and video which clearly explain why it is important to educate disabled children in mainstream schools. It discusses the issues that face teachers who want to include disabled children naturally in their school. From Comic Relief Education, Unit 2 Drywall Estate Castle Road Sittingbourne ME10 3RL.

AWAAZ: a video and booklet for Asian families with children with disabilities. Available in Bengali, English, Gujerati, Hindi, Panjabi and Urdu from the Council for Community Relations Elliot House 3 Jacksons Row Manchester M2 5WD.

BEING WHITE focuses on a group of men and women going through the process of looking at themselves as White people. Each has a different perspective but they all gradually realise how much authority and power they have just by virtue of their `Being White'. From: Battersea Studios Television, Thackeray Road, London SE8 4AG. Tel: 081 692 6322.

CAN MY CHILD BE HELPED? provides information and support for Asian parents whose children are disabled. It stresses the important role parents and family play in the child's development and achievement of full potential and encourages parents to ask questions of professionals. Available in Bengali, English, Gujarati, Hindi and Panjabi from CFL Vision PO Box 35 Wetherby LS23 7EX Tel: 01937 541083.

CHILDREN WITHOUT PREJUDICE: A VIDEO PACK designed for everyone involved with young children but especially for those who want ideas on putting the antiracist/multicultural aspects of the Children Act into practice. Notes for Trainers is included in the pack but is also a useful resource on its own. The exercises are suitable for in-service programmes and for education, care and social work courses. From the Early Years Trainers Anti-Racist Network PO Box 28 Wallasey L45 9NP Tel: 0151 639 6136.

CHOOSING CHILDMINDING outlines the elements which go to make up the complex role of the childminder and refers to the process of childminder registration, what this involves and highlights the support that the National Childminding Association offers. Available with commentary in Bengali, English, Gujarati, Hindi, Punjabi, Somali and Urdu. A booklet is included in the pack which is available from the National Childminding Association. 8 Masons Hill, Bromley BR2 9EY. Tel: 0181 464 6164.

COFFEE COLOURED CHILDREN: A young woman and her brother, who are of mixed parentage, talk about their feelings of growing up. Music and dreamy visual images contrast with hard hitting messages. A distressing and powerful video available from Battersea Studios Television, Thackeray Road, London SE8 4AG.

EARLY LITERACY EDUCATION WITH PARENTS is aimed at educators who wish to develop their work with parents to promote early literacy. It shows how children can learn about literacy from their families, and how nurseries/ schools work with parents to promote children's early literacy development. Filmed in home, neighbourhood and library settings, the video links current research with good practice. A manual, Preparing for Early Literacy Education with Parents designed for initial and in-service training courses includes suggestions for using the video, layouts for overhead transparencies and photocopiable hand-outs. The video and the manual are available from Sheffield University Television 5 Favell Road Sheffield S3 7QX.

EDUCATING THE WHOLE CHILD: This video and a book of the same name argues that the prevailing silencing and the invisibility of the child's cultural, racial and social identity in the learning environment lies at the heart of race, gender and class inequalities. From Equality Learning Centre 356 Holloway Road London N7 6PA Tel: 0171 700 8127.

PLAY FOR ASIAN PARENTS and CHILDREN: is sponsored by the Department of Health and produced by the Council of British Pakistanis in Birmingham highlights the importance of play for young children, the vital role of parents and relations and how Asian languages and culture form part of the play and learning process. Available in Hindi/Urdu, Bengali; Panjabi, Gujerati and English from N. Films 78 Holyhead Road Birmingham B21 0LH Tel: 0121 507 0341.

THROUGH THE GLASS CEILING is an animated fairy story but its theme of equal opportunity at work is firmly set in the real world. The narration by Alan Bennett is brilliant. Available from Leeds Animation Workshop 45 Bayswater Row Leeds LS8 5LF. Tel/fax: 0113 248 4997

A WORLD OF DIFFERENCE is an entertaining and thought provoking animated film which imaginatively raises issues around effective school practices. Available from Leeds Animation Workshop 45 Bayswater Row Leeds LS8 5LF. Tel/fax: 0113 248 4997

# Bibliography

Adler, S. (1993) Aprons and Attitudes: a consideration of feminism in children's books, in H. Claire, J. Maybin, and J. Swann, (eds) *Equality Matters: Case studies from the Primary School.* Clevedon: Multilingual Matters.

Adler, S. (1993) Great Adventures and Everyday Events, in M. Barrs and S Pidgeon (eds) *Reading the Difference.* London: Centre for Language in Primary Education.

Annan, M. (1993) From A Different Perspective, in M. Barrs and S Pidgeon (eds) *Reading the Difference.* London: Centre for Language in Primary Education.

Barry, S. (1989) *The Boy Who Wouldn't Speak.* Willowdale, ON: Annick Press.

Bee, H. (1992) *The Developing Child.* Sixth Edition. New York: HarperCollins.

Biggs, A. and Edwards, A. (1992) 'I Treat Them All The Same – Teacher-Pupil Talk in Multi-Ethnic Classrooms'. *Language and Education,* Vol 5, No 3.

Bourne, J. *Towards an Anti-Racist Feminism.* London: Institute of Race Relations.

Bradman, T. and Browne, E. (1988) *Through My Window.* London: Little Mammoth.

Brah, A. and Minhas, R. (1985) Structural Racism or Cultural Difference: schooling for Asian girls, in G. Weiner (ed.) *Just a Bunch of Girls.* Buckingham: Open University Press.

Brain, J. and Martin, M. (1983 ) *Childcare and Health.* second edition. London: Hulton Educational.

Brown, B. (1995) 'Whom Do We Include: do Irish and Jewish People suffer racism?' in *Nursery World* January.

Brown, B. (1994) 'Thinking it Over: the terminology of 'race'' in *Multicultural Teaching*, Vol 12, No 2.

Brown, C., Barnfield, J. and Stone, M. *Spanner In the Works.* (1990) Stoke on Trent: Trentham Books.

Browne, N. and France, P. (1985) Sexist Talk in the Nursery, in Gaby Weiner (ed.) *Just a Bunch of Girls.* Buckingham: Open University Press.

Burgess-Macey, C. and Crichlow, K. (1996) The Equal Opportunities Curriculum, in G. Blenkin and A. Kelly (eds) *Early Childhood Education.* London: Paul Chapman.

Carrington, B. and Troyna, B. (1988) (eds) *Children and Controversial Issues.* Lewes: The Falmer Press.

Claire, H. (1996) *Reclaiming Our Pasts: equality and diversity in the primary history curriculum* Stoke-on-Trent: Trentham Books

Coard, B. (1971) *How the West Indian Child is made Subnormal in the British School System.* London: New Beacon Books.

Connolly, P. (1994) Racism, Anti-Racism and Masculinity. Conference paper, 'International Sociology of Education Conference' University of Sheffield, January.

Coyle, J. (1996) My Trailer in *Stories from Travelling Children.* London: Haringey Traveller Education Service.

Cummins, J. (1984) 'Bilingualism and Special Education: issues in assessment and pedagogy'. Clevedon: *Multilingual Matters* 6.

Cummins, J. (1996) *Negotiating Identities: education for empowerment in a diverse society,* California Association for Bilingual Education. Available from Stoke-on-Trent: Trentham Books'.

Cummins, J. (1996a) 'Negotiating Identities in the Classroom and Society' in *Multicultural Teaching* vol 15, no1.

Das, P. (1993) *I is for India.* London: Frances Lincoln.

Davenport, G. (1988) *An Introduction to Child Development.* London: Unwin Hyman Ltd.

Derman-Sparks, L. (1989) *Anti-Bias Curriculum: tools for empowering young children.* Washington: National Association for the Education of Young Children.

Derman-Sparks, L. (1993) *Equality In Practice.* London: Early Years Trainers Anti-Racist Network and Save the Children.

Derman-Sparks, L. (1996), Being a White Anti-Racist, in *Travelling the Anti-Racist Road.* London: Early Years Trainers Anti-Racist Network.

Derman-Sparks, L. and Brunson-Phillips, C. (1997), *Teaching/Learning Anti-Racism: a developmental approach.* New York: Teachers College Press.

Doherty, B. (1992) *Snowy.* London: HarperCollins

Donaldson, M. (1978) *Children's Minds.* London: Fontana Press.

Douglas, J. (1967) *The Home and the School.* Panther Books.

Drummond, M, J, (1993) 'Learning About Gender Bias' in *Co-ordinate* Issue 33 January 1993.

Drummond, M, J, (1995) Observing Children in S. Smidts (ed.) *I Seed It and I Feeled It: young children learning.* University of North London Press.

Drummond, M, J, (1997) 'A Question of Quality: what sort of educators do our children deserve?' in *Reflections on Early Education and Care inspired by visits to Reggio Emilia, Italy.* London: British Association for Early Childhood Education.

Drury, R. (1997) Investigating Literacy in London in Gregory E. (ed.) *One Child, Many Worlds: Early learning in multicultural communities.* London: David Fulton

Dunn, J. (1988) *The Beginnings of Social Understanding.* Oxford: Blackwell.

Dunn, J (1993) *Young Children's Close Relationships: beyond attachment.* London: Sage.

Edwards, V. (1979) *The West Indian Language Issue in British Schools.* London: Routlege Kegan Paul.

Edwards, V. (1989) *Language and Disadvantage* (2nd Edition). London: Cole and Whurr

Edwards, V. (1995) *Speaking and Listening in Multicultural Classrooms.* Reading: The Reading and Language Information Centre.

Edwards, V. (1998) *The Power of Babel.* Stoke-on-Trent: Trentham Books.

Engel, D. and Whitehead, M. (1996) 'Which English? Standard English and Language Variety: some educational perspectives' *English in Education* Vol. 30, No1

Epstein, D. (1993) *Changing Classroom Cultures: anti-racism, politics and schools.* Stoke-on-Trent: Trentham Books.

Epstein, D. (1995) 'Girls Don't Do Bricks' in J. Siraj-Blatchford and I. Siraj-Blatchford. (Eds) *Educating the Whole Child.* Buckingham: Open University Press.

Etherington, J. (1993) *Integration In Practice. in Equality in Practice* London: Early Years Trainers Anti-Racist Network and Save the Children.

Eysenck, H. (1971) *Race, Intelligence and Education.* London: Temple Smith.

Faragher, J. and Glenda MacNaughton, G. (1990) *Working with Young Children.* Collingwood, Australia: TAFE Publications.

Faber, A. and Mazlish. E. (1996) *How to Talk so Kids can Learn at Home and in School.* New York: Simon and Schuster.

Fish Report (1985) *Educational Opportunities For All.* London: HMSO.

Flournoy, V. (1985) *The Patchwork Quilt.* London: The Bodley Head.

Foster, B. Equal Opportunities for Traveller Children in H. Claire, J. Maybin, and J. Swann, (eds) *Equality Matters: Case studies from the primary school.* Clevedon: Multilingual Matters

Gaine, B. and van Keulen, A. (1997) *Anti-Bias Training Approaches in the Early Years: a guide for trainers and teachers.* Utrecht: Agency Mutant and London: Early Years Trainers Anti-Racist Network.

Gaine, C. (1987) *No Problem Here: a practical approach to education and race in white schools.* London: Hutchinson.

Gaine, C. (1992) Why We Need an Anti-Racist Approach In Mainly White Areas, in *Racism a White Agenda.* London: Early Years Trainers Anti-Racist Network.

Garland, S. (1993) *Billy and Belle.* London: Puffin.

Gilborn, D. (1994) *Renewing Anti-Racism, Challenge, Change and Opportunity,* Runnymede Trust. Buckingham: Open University Press.

Gillborn, D. (1995) *Racism and Anti-Racism in Real Schools.* Buckingham: Open University Press.

Ginsburg, H. (1972) *The Myth Of The Deprived Child.* New Jersey: Prentice Hall.

Gregory, E. (1996) *Making Sense of a New World: learning to read in a second language.* London: Paul Chapman.

Grunsell, A. (1990) *Racism.* London: Franklyn Watts

Hazareesingh, S., Simms, K. and Anderson, P. (1989) *Educating the Whole Child: a holistic approach to education in early years.* London: Save the Children Building Blocks Educational.

Hewitt, R. (1996) *Routes of Racism: the social basis of racist action.* Stoke-on-Trent: Trentham Books.

Hoffman, M. (1991) *Amazing Grace*. London: Frances Lincoln.

Jeffcoate, R. (1979) *Positive Images: Towards a Multi-Racial Curriculum*. London: Writers and Readers Publishing Co-operative.

Jensen, A. (1969) *How much can we boost IQ and scholastic achievement?* Harvard Educational Review 39

Lane, J. (1996a) 'Acting On The Race Relations and The Children Act' in *Travelling the Anti-Racist Road*. London: Early Years Trainers Anti-Racist Network.

Lane, J. (1996b) *From Cradle To School*. London: Commission for Racial Equality.

Lindon, J. (1993) *Child Development From Birth: a practical focus*. London: National Children's Bureau.

Lloyd, B. (1987) Social Reconstructions of Gender in J. Bruner and H Haste, (eds) *Making Sense: the child's construction of the world*. London: Routledge.

Lloyd, B. and Duveen, G. (1992) *Gender Identities and Education*. Hemel Hempstead: Harvester Wheatsheaf.

Loewen, I. (1986) *My Mom is so Unusual*. Canada: Pemmican.

MacDonald, I., Bhavnani, R., Kahn, L., John, G. (1989) *Murder in the Playground: the report of the MacDonald enquiry into racism and racist violence in Manchester schools*. London: Longsight.

MacNaughton, G. (1995) Girls, Boys, and Race: where's the power? Conference paper, Washington National Association for the Education of Young Children, December.

Mathias, B. and French, M. A. (1996) *40 Ways To Raise A Nonracist Child*. New York: Harper-Collins.

McDonagh, M. (1996) Michael's Story in *Stories from Travelling Children* London: Haringey Traveller Education Service.

Milner, D. (1983) *Children and Race: Ten Years On*. London: Ward Lock Educational.

Morgan, G. (1996) 'An Investigation into the Achievement of African Caribbean pupils' *Multicultural Teaching*.

Mosely, J. (1993) *Turn Your School Around*. Wisbech: Learning Development Aids.

Moss, P. and Penn, H. (1996) *Transforming Nursery Education*. London: Paul Chapman.

Myers, K. (1985) 'Beware Of The Backlash' in *School Organisation* 5, 1.

Nottingham County Council (1991) Pupil Exclusion From Nottingham Secondary Schools.

Ofsted Report (1993) *Access and Achievement in Urban Education*. London: OFSTED Publications.

Ofsted Report (1996) *Recent Research on the Achievement of Ethnic Minority Pupils*. London: OFSTED Publications.

Ofsted Report (1996a) *The Education of Travelling Children*. London: OFSTED Publications.

Ogilvy, C. Boath, E. Cheyne, W. Jahoda, G. and Schaffer, H. (1990) 'Staff Attitudes and Perceptions in Multicultural Nursery Schools' in *Early Child Development and Care*, Volume 64.

Ogilvy C, Boath E, Cheyne W, Jahoda G and Schaffer H (1992) 'Staff-Child Interaction Styles in Multi-ethnic Nursery Schools' in the *British Journal of Development Psychology* Volume 10.

Onyefulu, I. *A is for Africa.* London: Frances Lincoln.

Patrick, P. and Burke, H. (1993) Equal Opportunities in H. Claire, J. Maybin, and J. Swann, (eds) *Equality Matters: Case studies from the primary school.* Clevedon: Multilingual Matters.

Piaget, J. (1977) *The Development of Thought. Equilibration of cognitive structures.* New York: The Viking Press.

Plowden Report (1967) London: HMSO.

Pugh, G. and Selleck, D. (1996) Listening to and Communicating with Young Children in R., Davie, G., Upton and V., Varma (eds) in *The Voice of the Child.* Lewes: Falmer Press.

Purkey, W. (1970) *Self-concept and School Achievement.* London: Paul Chapman.

Ramdeen, L, (1988) 'Primary Considerations' in *Multicultural Teaching* 6.2.

The Rampton Report (1981) *West Indian Children in our Schools.* London: HMSO

Reay, D. (1993) He Doesn't Like You Miss in Claire, H. Maybin, J. and Swann, J. (eds) *Equality Matters: case studies from the primary school.* Clevedon: Multilingual Matters.

Rieser, R. and Mason, M. (1990) *Disability Equality In The Classroom: a human rights issue.* London: Equality In Education.

Rosenthal, R. and Jacobsen, L. (1968) *Pygmalion In The Classroom.* New York: Holt, Rinehart and Winston.

Ross, A. (1995) Children In An Economic World, in J. Siraj-Blatchford, and I. Siraj-Blatchford, (eds) *Educating the Whole Child.* Buckingham: Open University Press.

Ross, C. and Browne, N.(1993) *Girls As Constructors In The Early Years.* Stoke-on Trent: Trentham Books.

Rumbold, A. (1990) *Starting With Quality*: report of the Committee of Inquiry into the quality of the educational experience offered to 3 and 4 year olds. London: Department of Education and Science.

Runnymede Trust (1997) *Islamphobia: the challenge for us all.* London: Runnymede Trust.

Rutter, J. (1994) *Refugee Children in the Classroom.* Stoke-on-Trent: Trentham Books.

Sandell, P. (1993) 'All My Selves' in *Coordinate* January Issue 33.

Schiller, C, (1974) cited by Shirley Maxwell in Preparation For Teaching in *Reflections on Early Education and Care* inspired by visits to Reggio Emilia, Italy. London: British Association for Early Childhood Education.

Scott, W. (1997) Foreword to *Reflections On Early Education And Care:* inspired by visits to Reggio Emilia, Italy. London: British Association for Early Childhood Education.

Siraj-Blatchford, I. (1991) Quality Care Is Anti-Racist Care in *Learning by Doing.* London: Early Years Trainers Anti-Racist Network.

Siraj-Blatchford, I. (1994) *The Early Years: laying the foundations for racial equality.* Stoke-on-Trent: Trentham Books.

Siraj-Blatchford, I. (1995) Racial Equality Education: identity, curriculum and pedagogy in J Siraj-Blatchford and I Siraj-Blatchford (Eds) *Educating the Whole Child*. Buckingham: Open University Press.

Skelton, C. (1988) Demolishing the House that Jack Built. in B. Carrington and B. Troyna (eds) *Children And Controversial Issues*. Lewes: Falmer Press.

Smikle, J. Moynihan, C. and des Vignes, L. (1997) One Vision. London: Save the Children'.

Smith, R. (1997) Guilty as charged: the price of talking Brummie. *The Independent*, 26 September.

Spafford, D. and Bolloten, B. (1995) 'The Admission and Induction of Refugee Children into School'. *Multicultural Teaching* Vol. 14 Number 1 Autumn 7-9.

Swann Report (1985) *Education For All. The Report of the Commission of Enquiry into the Education of Children from Ethnic Minority Groups*. London: HMSO.

Taylor, A. and Costley, D. (1995) Effective Schooling for All: the 'special educational needs' dimension in J. Siraj-Blatchford and I. Siraj-Blatchford (eds) *Educating the Whole Child*. Buckingham: Open University Press.

Tizard, B. and Hughes, M. (1984) *Young Children Learning: talking and thinking at home and at school*. Fontana: London.

Troyna, B. and Hatcher, R. (1992). *Racism in Children's Lives: a study of mainly white primary schools*. London: Routledge in association with the National Children's Bureau

Turner, M. (1997) Working in Partnership: parents, teacher and support teacher together in (ed.) Gregory E. *One Child, Many Worlds: Early learning in multicultural communities* London: David Fulton.

Vigna, J. (1989) *Black Like Kyra, White Like Me*. Niles, Whitman.

Vygotsky, L. (1978) *Mind In Society*. Cambridge Mass: Harvard University Press.

Weiner, G. (1985) Equal Opportunities, Feminism and Girls' Education: Introduction in (ed) G. Weiner *Just a Bunch of Girls*. Buckingham: Open University Press.

Weinraub, M. Clemens, L. Sockloff, A, Ethridge,T. Gracely, E. and Myers, B. (1984) 'The Development of Sex Role Stereotypes in the Third Year'. *Child Development*, 55.

Whalley, M. (1994) *Learning to be Strong: setting up a neighbourhood service for under-fives and their families*. London: Hodder and Stoughton.

Whalley, M. (1997) *Reflections On Early Education And Care: inspired by visits to Reggio Emilia, Italy*. London: British Association for Early Childhood Education.

Williams, J. and Best, D. (1990) *Measuring Sex Stereotypes: a multination study*. Newbury Park, C.A.: Sage.

Williams, V. A. (1983) *Chair for my Mother*. London: Julia MacRae.

Wood, D. and Wood, H. (1983) 'Questioning the Pre-school Child' in *Educational Review* 35, 2 149-162.

Wright, C. (1991) *Early Years Anti-Racist Practice Legislation and Research*. London: Early Years Trainers Anti-Racist Network.

Yates, D. (1996) *Making It Real: introducing a global dimension in the early years*. Birmingham: Development Education Centre.

Yeatman, A. (1988) *A Review of Multicultural Policies and Programs in Children's Services*. Canberra: Office of Multicultural Affairs: Australia.

# Index

This index includes subjects (excluding the book's major themes of racism and sexism) and authors. Book titles are indicated under the authors of children's books only.

ablism 1, 7, 64, 123

Adler, Sue 99

African-Caribbean people 30, 32-3, 44, 56, 77

American Declaration of Independence 137

Annan, Michael 33-4, 129

Asian people 43-4, 52-3, 96-7

    and language 77, 79, 84

    stereotypes of 4, 31-3

assessment 56

assimilation 34, 41, 97

Baldwin, James 122

Barry, Steve

    *The Boy Who Wouldn't Speak* 98

Bee, Helen 14

Best, Deborah 18

Biggs, A 55

bilingual assistants 79-82

Blyton, Enid 66

body language 12, 73, 84, 93

Bolloten, Bill 118

books

    and positive images 24, 98-100

Bradman, Tony and Eileen Browne

    *Through My Window* 99

Brain, Jean 31-2

British Empire 31

British Sign Language 39, 81

Brown, Clare 97-8

Browne, Eileen *see* Bradman, Tony and Eileen Browne

Browne, Naima 61, 73, 101

Brunson Phillips, Carol 82, 137

Burgess-Macey, Celia 43

Burke, Helena 15, 64

Carnegie Corporation 12

Children Act (1989) 103, 125, 135, 136

circle time 93-5

Claire, Hilary 100

collaboration

    and learning 4, 87, 91, 102

    with parents 103-6, 109-11, 116, 121

'colour-blind' approach 49, 54-5, 130

Commission for Racial Equality 135, 136

compensatory education 40-1

conflict management 112, 120, 133-5

Connolly, Paul 18

Costley, D 40

Coyle, James 61

Creole 70, 77

Crichlow, Kerry 43

Cummins, Jim 31, 74, 89, 136

curriculum 3-4, 37-8, 43-4, 51, 55, 78, 83, 85, 91, 104

    culturally appropriate 25, 46-7, 50, 110

    'hidden' 50